AROUND THE WORLD IN MANY WAYS

DAVID RICHARDSON

AROUND THE WORLD IN MANY WAYS

DAVID RICHARDSON

ISBN 9781914615580
A CIP catalogue record for this book is available from the British Library.

Published 2023
Tricorn Books,
Treadgolds
1a Bishop Street
Portsmouth
PO1 3HN

AROUND THE WORLD IN MANY WAYS

CONTENTS

My late wife Lorna who appears throughout the book

PROLOGUE

Readers of my autobiography *In at the Deep End* will have learned of my unexpected and accidental diversification from farming into broadcasting and writing. In that book I mentioned my trips abroad but skated over most of the details as I thought they would interfere with the rest of the story. But what follows is an account of some of the dozens of countries I have visited for work and for pleasure. Taking advice from Ernest Hemingway, who said *never write all that you know*, I have not recounted all of my experiences but selected the highlights and in some cases the lowlights of my many trips. For the record, they have all been enjoyable, usually at the time but sometimes in retrospect. I hope you enjoy them too.

Meanwhile, my gratitude to those who have made my travels possible, including the National Federation of Young Farmers Clubs, the BBC, Anglia TV, AgriTravel (now named Field Farm Tours), Farm Africa, my family and friends and all the people who have travelled with me wherever I have gone.

Bon voyage

David Richardson

INTRODUCTION

My first journey abroad was a school trip to Switzerland. It was in the summer of 1951. I was thirteen and the ten-day trip cost £39. The exchange rate then was about ten Swiss francs to the £1. We travelled by ferry and train across Holland and Germany to a small village on the northeast corner of Lake Lucerne called Brunen. The journey seemed endless. European trains weren't as fast then as they are now and some of my more agile school friends climbed in the luggage racks and pretended to sleep. The schoolteachers who accompanied us seemed pretty relaxed about our behaviour so long as we didn't break anything. One was a man and the other a woman. We deduced later that they were more interested in one another than they were with us and we got away with all sorts of mischief once we had worked out their relationship.

We stayed in a pub/guest house called Gastof Neuwirt which we were told could be interpreted as Guest House New Landlord. We slept four to a room under new-fangled things called duvets (they hadn't arrived in Britain then) and these provided great ammunition one night when we had been on the schnapps (unsupervised) and decided to have a pillow fight. When the maid came in next morning she found feathers all over the floor and we got a dressing down from the teachers.

There was an unheated swimming pool in the village which we used a lot once we became acclimatised to the cold and I noticed the local girls who shared the pool with us had hairy armpits. I suspect Swiss women have caught up with the rest of the world by now but they hadn't then. We climbed the local mountain, took photographs with our Box Brownies and generally had a great time. And so did our pair of teachers.

Two years later as I was getting ready to leave school I joined another trip to Austria. This time the destination was Axams, near Innsbruck. Once again it was summer and we went by North Sea ferry and train. And perhaps being two years older I was a bit more observant. It was only a few months after the great tidal flood of January 1953 during which hundreds of Dutch people were drowned (and a lot of English people too, many of them in Norfolk). And I remember seeing the tide marks halfway up houses as we passed them on the train. I also remember the bomb damage across Germany as we flashed through towns that had been targeted by allied raids. It was, after all, only a few years after the Second World War and reparations were only just beginning.

Axams was a lovely little village with a fast-running stream through the middle of it and we enjoyed getting to know the locals as far as our fractured German allowed. Near to the guesthouse where we stayed was a pub with a bowling alley where we spent many happy hours. And on the Saturday afternoon the local oompah band came and played for dancing. We British teenaged boys had little idea of how to dance but the local girls were keen to teach us and we didn't take much persuasion to join them on the outdoor dance floor. One of them, called Monika, seemed to take a bit of a shine to me (and I to her) and we had lots of innocent fun together that week.

The author aged 16 with Monika

And so was born my desire to travel, enhanced by my parents' love of exploring Britain. As a child I had joined them on motoring tours of Scotland, the north of England and Devon and Cornwall. In my late teens I read many books about different parts of the world. I had an uncle who served in the RAF who was, for a time, based in Ceylon, now renamed Sri Lanka. He wrote to me regularly describing the places where he lived. It seemed to me that the world was a big place and that I should do my best to learn more about it.

So, when the opportunity to apply to visit Canada through a Young Farmers Club exchange scheme was announced at our local club I decided to have a go. The system was to have interviews at county level to see whether you were a suitable candidate or not, and then, if the panel deemed you worthy, to go to Cambridge for regional assessment. I passed the Norfolk grilling and went to Cambridge where I thought I had a good chance. But after all the interviews had been completed I was told I had not been chosen. To say I was disappointed would be an understatement. However, as I was packing up to go home, I was called back into the interview room. The chairman told me they had been impressed by my presentation but that they had chosen a girl who was twenty-five ahead of me for that reason. But they encouraged me to apply again the following year.

Six months later I was successful in hiring a 260-acre farm. It, obviously, had to come first so I did not re-apply to go on an exchange visit. That, it seemed to me, was the end of my ambition to travel. I could not see how other opportunities would present themselves so I got my head down and tried to make a go of the farm. Little did I know that there would be multiple opportunities in the years that followed.

This book is a light-hearted account of some of the countries I have since visited, interspersed with a few of the insights I have learned that I wouldn't have if I'd stayed at home.

HOLLAND

The farm was in a poor state when I took the tenancy, with poor drainage and an infestation of twitch on every field, but I still managed to stay involved with the Young Farmers Club at Wymondham. They had elected me to the Norfolk County Executive Committee and that committee had elected me as its chairman. After my year in the chair was over, I was asked to represent Norfolk on the National Council of Young Farmers which met a couple of times a year in its London office. YFC HQ was at that time 55 Gower Street, just off Russell Square. I decided that two days in London per year was doable so agreed to serve.

After one Council meeting in early 1962, Barbara Tyldon, the staff official who coordinated exchange visits, took me on one side and asked if I would lead a tour to Holland. It would consist of twenty young farmers from across the country; we would each stay with hosts who worked for or were associates of Vicon, the hay turner manufacturers, who were sponsoring the ten-day tour.

The tour was scheduled for the following May and my wife, Lorna, was expecting our second child in mid-June. I could probably be spared from the farm. It was not a particularly busy time of year on a mainly arable system. But what about the timing and the expected baby? I told Barbara I could not give her an answer right away and that I would have to discuss it with Lorna.

Knowing how frustrated I had been to miss out on the Canadian trip a few years previously she said I should accept. I'd be back a month before the expected birth so no problem. I also had to ask my father, with whom I was now in partnership. He too encouraged me to do it and said he and my mother would keep an eye on Lorna. I think he felt a vicarious pride in my achievements. So, with their blessing, I phoned Barbara to say I would lead the party.

We flew from Southend Airfield which, at the time, was a grass strip, in a converted Dakota bomber. Most of the party, including me, had never flown before so it was with a fair bit of trepidation that we boarded the old aircraft. How many bombing raids over Germany it had survived we didn't know but the pilot, complete with a moustache that was probably a hangover from the RAF and the war, was a breezy fellow and full of confidence. Pilots weren't locked away from passengers in those days and we could see every manoeuvre he made.

After a bit of a bumpy ride across the North Sea we landed as scheduled at Rotterdam. There to greet us was Piet Vogelaar, our guide and interpreter for the next ten days and the head of marketing for Vicon. I was to stay with Piet and his wife Bepe in the village of Nieuw-Vennep, close to Amsterdam and almost alongside Schiphol Airport. Vicon's factory was in the village and it was the first stop on our tour.

We saw how the iconic hay turners were made and also a prototype spading machine, designed to replicate the actions of a man with a spade. I suspect it was one of the forerunners of minimal cultivation but I don't think it was ever adopted outside of Holland.

It was a packed tour during which we learned that one third of Holland was below sea level, including the polder where we were staying. Originally the land was drained by windmills, the remains of which were still maintained as museum pieces. But as soon as pumps could be powered mechanically and the water levels didn't have to rely on wind power, the Dutch installed a steam engine. We were taken to see it and guess what – the steam engine was made in Devon. The theory was that steam power had been developed for Cornish tin mines and pragmatic Dutch engineers had sought the best they could get to run their pumps.

We went to see the Zuiderzee, an inland sea created by damming a shallow bay to the northeast of most of Holland and south of Friesland. Hence the translation 'South Sea' relates to the province of Friesland. The dam was about 30 miles long, was called the Afsluitdijk and had a road along it. We travelled that road and it led us to Flevoland, a new polder made possible by draining part of the Zuiderzee to expose the land beneath.

Some of the new land was allocated to agriculture, some to nature, and some to new towns, like Leylystad. The farming land was managed by the Dutch government for a few years while it was laser levelled, drained and cropped with plants that tolerated any remaining salt before handing it over to farmers who had to have an agriculture degree to be eligible to farm. Lelystad was still not finished when we were there and put me in mind of Aldous Huxley's *Brave New World*. But I dare say it has matured now after all these years.

One farm that had already been developed on Flevoland was called Flevohof. It was designed as an educational farm to demonstrate what farming was about. There were livestock units with pigs and cows and a milking parlour with windows to allow visitors to see what was happening. There were greenhouses full of various plants like tomatoes and peppers and even back then they were showing how insects could be used to control other insects and bees could be employed to pollinate plants. Many years later I was privileged to be invited to the Koppert company, near Rotterdam. Its founder was one of the originators of insect control of pests and pollination and it was instructive to learn how advanced techniques had become. Arable farming was demonstrated too with ploughs and drills and people available to describe what they did and why. We were impressed and I remember coming home and saying to all who would listen that we should do something similar in Britain. But nobody was listening at the time. Sadly, however, it was poorly supported by Dutch people and went bust. I understand it is now an amusement park. An example, perhaps, of urbanisation affecting Holland as much as it does the UK.

One demonstration farm, or perhaps garden would be more accurate, that we visited which is still operating was the Keukenhof, or kitchen garden where thousands of tulips were in full bloom. We walked through the paths and lawns between the tulip beds and there were tulips of every colour imaginable. And beyond the garden were whole fields with the same kind of colourful variation. It was beautiful and a few years later I took Lorna back there so she could share my delight in the place.

Still on the theme of flowers, we Young Farmers were taken to the Aalsmeer clock auction where flowers were pushed through on numbered trolleys in front of buyers who sat at desks punching buttons to stop a clock whose hand swung backwards from a high to a low price. It was so quick we could not understand how the buyers could judge what they were bidding for. But then we weren't familiar with the system. The clock auction has now grown to be the biggest flower auction in the world attracting blooms from countries such as Africa, South America and even Russia. There is direct access to Schiphol Airport through underground tunnels and many of the buyers these days are purchasing to re-export – to Britain for instance. I was back there a few years ago and it was mind-boggling.

We Young Farmers also went to Leeuwarden, the capital of Friesland and home of the Dutch Friesian cow. There, in the town square was a bronze statue of the kind of cow that had made the area famous. But back in 1962 dairy farming was pretty basic compared with today. We saw cows being milked out on pastures that were divided by little canals. We saw one cow being brought back from its pasture standing in a boat as the farmer punted it home. There were very few herds of more than a dozen or two and we were amazed that this cottage industry had produced cattle that had spread across the world.

But the Dutch are born traders, situated as they are at the mouth of three big rivers – the Rhine, the Meuse and the Ijssel. Most of them speak at least three languages – Dutch, German and English – and do so fluently, which gives them a big advantage when doing deals. This was illustrated when I went with my host, Piet Vogelaar (which means bird catcher by the way), to visit his father's farm. The old man showed me around, all 120 acres of it, the far end of which butted up against the runway of Schiphol Airport. He grew potatoes, sugar beet and wheat and the land was clearly fertile and easy working. The fields were all in one block and surrounded by small canals that were totally parallel as they had been marked out when the polder was created from the sea.

Then we went into his 'Dutch' barn. It was one big building divided up into areas for potato storage and grain storage with another for machinery, of which there was a lot. He had two tractors, a combine, a potato harvester, a potato planter, a sugar beet harvester, a sugar beet drill, a corn drill, a roll and sundry cultivators. I smiled to myself as I added up the cost of all these machines. Admittedly they weren't all new but even so he had well above what he could really justify. I felt slightly superior management wise as we walked into the farmhouse for a cup of coffee.

As we drank our coffee, old man Vogelaar spoke to his son in Dutch. And Piet translated for me. "My father is rather concerned about a ship load of grain he's bought from America. The ship is delayed by bad weather and the people he's sold the grain on to are running short of supplies." I felt about an inch high and glad I hadn't shared my thoughts about the old man's business acumen. And I wondered how many 120-acre farmers in Britain were in the habit of buying and selling ship loads of grain from America.

As is clear from the above, I have been back to Holland many times since that first trip. And I have developed a deep affection and respect for the country and its people. On subsequent trips I have seen how Dutch farmers have increased their production of pigs and dairy products as well as potatoes and horticultural produce like tomatoes and peppers. To be honest, their business instincts have led them to overdo it in some respects. Their expansion of intensive livestock has led to greater quantities of slurry and associated smells. One of the problems is that most of the intensification occurs in the southeast and most of the crops that need organic manure are grown in the northwest.

I've filmed some of the schemes they have devised to correct this anomaly for UK TV farming programmes. Like transporting slurry from where it is produced to where it can be spread on land. But slurry is heavy, expensive and rather unpleasant to move long distances. So they decided to try to separate the solids from the liquid so that the solids would be much reduced in weight and the liquids could be pumped into one of Holland's rivers without polluting. We filmed that plant too. It was a massive investment and we weren't sure who had paid for it. Probably the Dutch government. Anyway, the solids were being efficiently separated and sent off for fertiliser while the liquids were filtered several times through a series of aerating tanks until, finally, they were purified and fit to drink. Or that was what the management claimed. Indeed, they had a photograph in their office of Queen Beatrix when she came to declare the plant open, drinking a glass of the purified slurry/water. They challenged me to do the same for our cameras but I'm afraid I declined.

Urban frustration at the same problem, especially the smell, has recently persuaded the Dutch government to threaten to buy large chunks of land by compulsory purchase and take it out of farming altogether. Holland is one of the most densely populated countries in the world and the townspeople have rebelled against the farmers, despite the fact that food accounts for a large proportion of the country's export income. The farmers have reacted to these threats by blocking roads with their tractors and starting their own political party which has quickly become a real force in the country.

Who will win? Who knows? But as I have seen over the sixty years I've been watching them, Dutch farmers are not to be messed with. They've built thriving businesses from small beginnings, often through cooperatives. They can produce and they can market. I wouldn't bet against them.

And many's the time I think back to that first visit in 1962; about the welcome we received, some of it based on what our soldiers did in helping to release them from the German occupation. I've been to Arnhem where many British soldiers are buried and the Dutch treat those graves with reverence and care. And I've seen the bridge that provided the title for Richard Attenborough's film *A Bridge Too Far.*

On a more secular note, I remember, back then, being introduced to *potat frites* – chips to us Brits, served with mayonnaise. Delicious. And Dutch restaurants where the waiters are almost always men dressed in black jackets and striped trousers, with impeccable manners. You almost feel they should be dining and you should be waiting on them.

USA

I first went to America in 1973. It was an exciting time to be there. The UK was just getting used to joining the Common Market (later re-christened the EU) and the then president, Jimmy Carter, had banned the export of soya beans to Europe because of a US domestic shortage. But that was not the reason for the trip.

ICI, then one of the leading suppliers of products such as fertilisers and chemicals to UK farmers, had recently launched a contact weedkiller called Gramoxone (remember?) and they wanted to publicise it. It was already being used widely in America and ICI's publicity department was tasked with getting the product better known in this country.

The company offered to take a small group of agricultural journalists to the States to see how farmers there were using it. I happened to be writing a few columns for farm magazines and presenting the weekly Radio 4 programme *On Your Farm* at the time and Tony Parkin, its producer and I were both invited to join the group.

We flew to Washington, arriving on a hot July day, and had time to do a bit of sightseeing before our Gramoxone tour began. The White House; the British Embassy with a statue of Churchill in the garden; Arlington Cemetery where JFK is buried beneath an eternal flame and so on.

Then our leader, Ian Allen, Head of PR for ICI, heard that Petrus Lardinois, then the Agriculture Commissioner of the Common Market, was in town to try to get the soya bean ban lifted and that he was to hold a press conference at the magnificent Washington Press Club that afternoon. Contacts were made, strings were pulled and as if by magic we were invited to the event. That kind of contact with someone in the eye of a storm doesn't happen often and we were grateful that ICI had made it happen even though it had nothing to do with their project. Quite apart from getting a bit of a scoop by interviewing

Lardinois, I met the editor of the *American Farm Journal* which later led to an invitation to write columns about British and European farming for her magazine. As the fertiliser distributor ad said – my fame was spreading.

Unexpected copy filed overnight, we set off to look at farms. The first was a mixed arable and dairy farm milking 200 cows. It was run by two brothers and was clearly a well-run enterprise. We asked our questions about their use of Gramoxone and how it allowed 'no-till' farming – the first time I had heard the phrase. I did an interview with the pair of them towards the end of which I threw in a question on how they divided responsibilities. "Gee, that's easy," said one of them. "To make sure we don't fight over the management I run the farm one year and he runs it the next."

Before we left for our next appointment Ian Allen asked Tony Parkin to propose a vote of thanks. On the way over in the plane he had asked each of us to buy a bottle of duty-free whisky to present to our American hosts. Tony duly obliged, saying how interesting we'd found the farm and handed one of the brothers a bottle of whisky. To which the response was, "Gee that's awful kind of you but our religion don't allow us to consume alcohol." Tony was embarrassed as we all were, but they kept the whisky!

What we hadn't realised was that we had come south of Washington and were in the Bible Belt. In the hotel we stayed in that night behind the reception desk were posters advertising about twenty different churches in the immediate area, all a little bit different from one another and all with slightly different interpretations of how to worship and codes of conduct. Meanwhile, our leader realised he'd boobed and dug into his suitcase for some spare ICI neckties he'd brought from Britain so that at the next farm we visited we wouldn't be similarly embarrassed.

That next farm was all arable and a bit hilly. The farmer told us how important it was not to disturb the soil when drilling his corn (maize) because he had such heavy rainstorms from time to time and loose soil would be eroded and washed into a nearby stream. He was direct drilling (a phrase we were just beginning to use at home) or, as he put it, no-till, across the slope on the contour of his fields and avoided cultivating up and down any slope for similar reasons.

He also told how he mixed different chemicals in his sprayer to minimise the number of times he sprayed. He was mixing weedkiller and insecticide with liquid fertiliser as the carrier. I asked him how he knew the various chemicals would be safe to mix. "Well," he said, "I pour a little of each into a bucket and stir it and if it don't explode I go ahead."

It seemed to us a rather crude and slapdash way of going to work but, as we later learned, it was typical of the approach of many American farmers.

But it was time to leave the farm and once again a member of our group had been asked to do a vote of thanks and present an ICI tie to our host (no whisky – we were still in the Bible Belt). At the end of his short speech our colleague handed him the tie in appreciation of his hospitality. "Well," he said, "that's real kind. But my religion don't allow me to wear a necktie."

It was a sharp introduction to American farmers and their beliefs, at least those in the south of the country and the Bible Belt. Yes, they're religious and that's fine. But some of the ways in which they express that religion is illogical and, in my opinion, ridiculous. Our trip and visits to farms continued and we never embarrassed ourselves again. Someone said thank you to our hosts and we left without giving them a present. But I sometimes think of those Bible Belt farmers these days as I hear of Donald Trump being first elected and then the favoured candidate for re-election as US president and I wonder how many Americans are like them.

A few days later we experienced the kind of rain some of our farmer hosts had talked about. We were in Norfolk, Virginia for some reason that I can't remember. Our bus driver looked to the sky and said over his loudspeaker, "Hi folks, I think we're gonna get a storm. I'm just gonna park up till it passes over." He found a nearby parking place on high ground and we waited. It wasn't long before the rain started and then thunder and lightning like I had never experienced before. The rain was so heavy that we could hardly see out of the bus windows and although we were on a high, flat park the water built up inches deep all around us. Then, suddenly, through the rain-washed windows we saw lightning strike a building about fifty yards away. The strike burned every electric wire in the building. It was like fireworks spreading through every room and the most frightening natural phenomenon

I had ever seen. "Is it going to get us next?" asked one of our group in a shaky voice. "No, we'll be OK," said the driver. "We got rubber tyres."

The whole episode seemed endless although it was only an hour. And when it was over we set off for New York. What we'd experienced confirmed the problem of soil erosion we'd heard about from farmers nearby better than any film or book. The following day I read in a New York newspaper, in a tiny piece near the end of the news section, that the previous day Norfolk, Virginia had a cyclone that didn't touch down and that 5.4 inches of rain had fallen in just over an hour.

Ian Allen from ICI was a bit of a history buff so we were able to share his passion as, on the way north to New York, we called at Gettysburg, where Abraham Lincoln gave his famous speech about "government of the people, for the people, by the people", defining democracy. He was also assassinated there. And we called at Williamsburg, the site where early European settlers lived and which today is a living museum and people walk around in clothes that were current in the 18th century and the old houses are preserved for posterity.

In New York we stayed at the Algonquin Hotel where Dorothy Parker, the socialite and wit, used to hold court. It was a Sunday afternoon and it was hot and humid but I was fascinated by the skyscrapers and the geometrically straight streets with ninety-degree junctions. We didn't have such things in England in 1973. And I went for a walk despite having been warned of the danger. I found Times Square and Fifth Avenue and eventually got back to the hotel safely and the next day we all flew home to Heathrow.

A few years later I was back in America again. This time it was at the behest of the managing director of the cooperative Eastern Counties Farmers. I was, at the time, Chairman of Loddon Farmers, one of a handful of requisite grain, potato and pig coops across East Anglia. But ECF was the biggest and Tom Thomas, an evangelistic Welshman, who ran it had visions of pulling all these smaller operations under the ECF umbrella. "That's what they do in America," he said, "so why can't we do it here?" And he put forward an argument to the chairmen of all the coops in the region that we should go there and see for ourselves – "and bring your wives too."

We discussed the proposal around the Loddon Farmers board table and my colleagues thought I should go. But I was sceptical from the start. I'd seen too many cooperative failures as I had toured the country making TV programmes for the BBC *Farming* programme. But it promised to be a good jolly and eventually I agreed to join the party. But I asked that my modest chairman's salary be used to pay the cost for myself and my wife and I would forego any further reward for the year in question. The Loddon board agreed and off we went.

This time we flew into Atlanta where an enormous cooperative called Goldkist was based. A great deal of its activities were based around chickens and eggs and it seemed to control every farm in the state of Georgia and beyond. Indeed, when we analysed it we realised that the business was essentially running vertically integrated production units. In other words, the coop owned the birds and supplied the feed and the farmers were like employees feeding the birds and collecting the eggs. The coop sold the chickens and the eggs and processed the chicken carcasses but the farmers saw little of the cash from those activities. It was mainly swallowed up by the administration of the coop. I judged it to be a nice business for the managers and the handful of farmers who served on the board but not for the people who did most of the work.

Tom Thomas was a bit of a trad jazz fan, as am I. So I was thrilled that we took a side trip to New Orleans. There was music everywhere – as you walked down the streets you heard it coming from every doorway. One evening my wife, Lorna, and I went to a club where a trumpeter called Al Hirt was the star attraction. He was up there with Louis Armstrong and nearly made that trumpet talk. We ordered local food which was pretty spicy and drank huge glasses of a punch, called schoners, a slightly alcoholic beverage. We loved it.

Jazz break over, we headed to Kansas, the home of yet another enormous cooperative called Farmland. It too spread its operation across a number of US states and it covered virtually every farming activity. It bought and sold grain, fertilisers, animal feeds, chemical sprays and so on and had a turnover of many hundreds of millions of dollars. Once again it had an impressive headquarters, which indicated little restraint of expenditure but every sign of providing an impressive and comfortable base for the administrators of the business.

Back home we were constantly conscious of holding costs down so that our operations benefited our members as much as possible, so this was a new experience for most of us.

But we couldn't fault the administrators and board members for their welcome and readiness to share their data. They were also generous in their hospitality and one evening they took us to a baseball game. Their team was the Kansas City Royals and we had front seats in the cooperative's own box. It was a new experience for us East Anglian yokels. Every time the local team scored fountains spurted up beside the scoreboard and a fanfare blared on the loudspeakers. I've forgotten who won the game but could not help thinking it was a bit like rounders that we had played in the primary school playground.

To finish the tour we went to a third coop near Syracuse, north of New York. It had a similar structure to the previous two that we'd visited but didn't seem as big or as dominant. But perhaps we were becoming used to the scale of things in the States. I do remember the ladies on the tour, including my wife Lorna, took a side trip to Niagara Falls one day while we men were shown yet another impressive head office and visited some of the members.

It was an interesting tour and I had lots to tell my Loddon Farmers board members when we returned. But nothing ever came of Tom Thomas's vision to take us all over. And some years later, after Tom Thomas had retired, Eastern Counties Farmers went bust. Meanwhile, some of the smaller coops in the region, including Loddon, thrived and then merged while avoiding the kind of extravagance we had seen in America. I don't think East Anglian farmers would tolerate what went on over there where it seemed to me the coops were managed more for the employees than for the farmer members.

I recently looked up the names of the three coops we visited on that tour on Google and couldn't find any of them. Maybe the farmer members had cottoned on to the fact that they were paying a handful of administrators who enjoyed an extravagant way of life but were ripping them off? I don't know. It may be they have just merged with others and become bigger still but that their names have been changed. It was forty years ago so all sorts of things may have happened. But like ECF, those US coops have disappeared.

My next visit to America was more domestic. It was to attend my eldest son, Andrew's, wedding in North Dakota. When he left agricultural college I suggested to him that a bit of travelling would be a good idea before he settled down. He agreed and after a few phone calls to friends ended up getting a job working for an irrigation company based in Colorado. They were setting up center pivot irrigation plants in the Texas panhandle and Nebraska and farming the land under them for investors. Andrew started as a dogsbody but it wasn't long before he was offered a regular job managing the crops under the irrigators which he clearly enjoyed, especially when he found a girlfriend. Rose's father had a farm in North Dakota and it seemed like a perfect match. He popped the question, she said yes, and off we went with about thirty Norfolk friends to attend their wedding.

We flew Canadian Airways from Norwich via Amsterdam to Winnipeg. This, you will appreciate, landed us in Canada but Winnipeg is a couple of hours' drive due north of Grand Forks in North Dakota and it seemed like the best way to reach our destination. The journey was OK except that three of our cases, including mine with my wedding suit inside it, did not get taken off the plane at Winnipeg but went on to Calgary. Fortunately we had travelled a few days early so that we could take a look at farming in North Dakota. But it took three days before we were reunited with our clothes and it was July and it was hot. I got through quite a lot of Lorna's deodorant in those three days.

I had asked Rose to arrange for our wedding party to look at North Dakota agriculture and she did a good job. We visited a couple of her uncle's farms, the Fargo Show that happened to be on at the time – just a small show but worth seeing – and also the Red River Valley, famous for potatoes. Among our party were a few specialist potato growers and as we walked across a field almost fit to harvest they were gobsmacked to find plants smothered with Colorado beetles. They'd eaten most of the leaves but they didn't appear to have reduced the yield much or the quality of the tubers. To put that experience into perspective, Colorado beetles were and are still regarded as the worst possible pest on a potato crop in the UK and to be avoided at all costs. But here were potato growers who seemed totally relaxed about the infestation. Amazing.

The wedding day dawned. Lorna and I were staying at her family's timber farmhouse and several family members had visited the previous day in anticipation of the wedding. The ancient plumbing could not cope with the extra use and as Lorna and I prepared for the midday ceremony we were shocked to see out of the bedroom window Rose's father on the lawn with the lavatory in pieces. He got it back together again in time to change his clothes, but it was a lesson in self-sufficiency. Out there in rural America where he had grown up you were miles from service industries and if your car broke down, or if your lavatory got blocked, as in this case, you mended it yourself.

The wedding took place in the Catholic church in the one-horse town that gloried in the title 'the City of Michigan, population 273' according to the city signs. We men in our dark suits were sweating like pigs in the heat. Ladies in their open-necked silk creations were a little more comfortable. And Rose, along with her bunch of bridesmaids who were old school friends, looked as cool as cucumbers.

The ceremony was conducted by an aging priest whose hobby was betting on horses, as his address to the bride and groom made clear. Then, as clouds began to gather, on to the reception in the nearby two-horse town of Lakota where there was a public hall big enough to accommodate the wedding party. We'd scarcely sat down when rain started falling, accompanied by violent lightning and thunder. We were all under cover but the rain was so severe that the local farmers, some of whom were Rose's uncles, were concerned about crop damage.

As we consumed the wedding breakfast, three elderly ladies appeared on the stage and started playing their instruments. One was on the upright piano, another had a zither and the third played a set of drums. To be honest they looked like an extended version of Hinge and Bracket but their music was rhythmic and fantastic. And as rain continued to fall, the local sheriff, complete with a star on his chest and a gun on his hip, came and stood in the lobby. Whether he was sheltering or keeping an eye out in case of trouble we couldn't tell. But there he stood through the speeches and the dancing afterwards without saying a word.

We'd got to know a few of Rose's uncles during the previous few days. They farmed around the same area and when we met them first, we detected a bit of nervousness. We were, after all, the friends and family of a foreign young man seeking to marry one of their daughters. But that didn't last long. As soon as we began talking farming they realised that we were just the same as them. That we had the same sort of problems with the weather, with the government, with supermarkets and so on.

But we also came to realise how insulated they were from the rest of the world. None of them had a passport and their knowledge of the world virtually stopped at the borders of North Dakota. Very few of the people we met at that wedding had been to Chicago, the nearest major city, and when they heard that some of us had been to New York and Washington they were almost in awe of us. The TV news broadcasts in the UK about happenings in Hollywood and New York are not the real America we saw in the Midwest. Mass shootings apart, those news items mainly concern the east and west coasts where most of the people live but we seldom hear much about the middle, nor they of us.

After their wedding, Andrew and Rose moved about a bit, finally settling in Denver, Colorado. Lorna and I visited them there a few times and also went skiing with them in Vail, only a three-hour drive from that 'mile-high city'. We'd done most of our skiing in the European Alps and the wide pistes of Vail were a new experience. While most European ski resorts feature narrow paths often between trees, Vail pistes were like skiing down a motorway. The manners of American skiers were different too. Whereas in Austria or Switzerland queues to get on lifts require sharp elbows at times, in America skiers say, "After you" and stand back to allow you in. And if someone is judged to be skiing recklessly – i.e. dangerously – the ski police patrols confiscate their ski pass.

Andrew and Rose produced a daughter, Ashley, on October 15th, 1987. Lorna had agreed to go to America to be with them and help Rose with baby care for the first few weeks after she was born. That morning Andrew rang to say things were happening a little earlier than expected and could Lorna come now. It was a Thursday and I managed to get a seat for her on a plane from Gatwick to Dallas early the following morning. That evening I drove her down to the Post House hotel beside Gatwick Airport ready for her early morning flight.

Having reached the hotel and settled, Lorna and I decided, since it was getting windy and there was a double bed in the room, that I would stay the night and set off back to Norfolk the following morning. I had to record the *Farming Diary* programme at 11am, ready for transmission the following Sunday, at Anglia TV studio so I knew it would mean an early start. I set an alarm clock for 6am and went to sleep. The double glazing on the hotel windows meant that I did not hear the wind becoming ever more fierce.

The alarm went off as scheduled and I began to dress. Suddenly the lights went out, leaving me feeling for my clothes in a strange room and talking to Lorna in the dark. I left the room reminding her to catch the bus to the terminal in time for her flight. Carefully I found my way down the stairs only to see a crowd of frustrated passengers waiting in the lobby. I heard someone say some flights had been cancelled but rushed out to the car park ready to drive to Norwich.

It was blowing a gale and there were trees down in the car park but I drove round them and set off north along the M23. It was only when I switched on the radio that I realised I was in the middle of the biggest gale in living memory. My trip to Norwich was clearly not going to be straightforward but I was obsessed with making it on time and pressed on. Parts of the motorways were littered with fallen trees but the carriageways were wide enough to let me past and I made it along the M23 around the M25 and up the M11, until I got to Barton Mills. There the M11 stopped and I could not continue along the single carriageway A11 because a sign said the road was closed because of fallen trees.

I had no alternative but to try the Swaffham road which appeared to be open. But I hadn't gone many miles along that tree-lined road when I saw a tree starting to fall across it. I accelerated and saw it fall in my mirror. I pressed on and had to double back a few times and find a new way to reach my destination. Mobile phones had not been invented by then and I was sure all the landlines would be out because of fallen trees. So, I had not been able to contact my colleagues at Anglia. But I walked into the studio at five to eleven to find the researcher on the programme panicking because he had been told to present the programme in my absence. Fortunately I had written the script the day before and all was well. I managed to do my job.

Lorna eventually got to Dallas having caught the first plane out of Gatwick on Friday afternoon. She was diverted via New York where she changed planes but was treated magnificently by the air hostesses when they knew she was on her way to "become a grandma". They forwarded her identity to her next change of plane and she said she was treated like royalty as they speeded her passage through airports. And Andrew met her at her last stop wearing a Stetson. He'd gone native and she hardly recognised him. Interestingly, Ashley is now a flight attendant with Virgin Air.

In the autumn of 1990, I was asked by Zeneca, a subsidiary of ICI, if I would go to Memphis, Tennessee, to give a talk to a bunch of American agriculturalists about sustainable farming. I was promised a Club Class seat on the plane and agreed to do it. Zeneca's invitation was based on some columns I had written in the now defunct *Big Farm Weekly* and I suppose they hoped my words would replicate their company policy.

My theme for my talk was that sustainability in farming had many meanings and many interpretations and I mentioned a few of them – the use of crop rotations to avoid disease affecting crops or the soil; care for the soil itself to avoid damaging the most important raw material a farmer has; care for the environment and other creatures that depend on it, and those, like insects, that are beneficial to farming and so on.

But, I said, the one interpretation that could not be disputed was that farming must be profitable, because if it were not it would not exist at all and then where would our food come from. I concluded that farmers must adopt systems of farming that combined all of these objectives and only then could their operations be termed sustainable.

My talk seemed to go down well and several members of the audience congratulated me for saying what few in America accepted at the time. On the flight home I sat next to the man from Zeneca who had persuaded me to give the talk. As the canapés came round for Club Class passengers he said, "Thank you David. I liked what you said. But what are you going to do about it?"

I knew that we had a six-hour flight ahead of us so I told him. For the previous ten years I had been trying to persuade the captains of industry in the UK to do something about the bad press farmers were getting. We had been blamed for poisoning birds and insects with sprays that we were accused of drenching on our land. Our use of artificial fertilisers had been described almost as a criminal act. But we were the victims in all this. Farmers used these products on the recommendation of firms like his and we got blamed. Whereas those who manufacture them and push them onto farmers escaped almost scot-free.

I told him that I had had similar conversations with the big firms' bosses as I had visited them while making TV and radio programmes and I had told them they should modify their recommendations and get together to support an organisation to correct press exaggeration and advocate a more nature-friendly approach. The response had always been, "We can't possibly cooperate with our competitors and in any case we have public relations departments to deal with that sort of thing."

He listened quietly to my rant. And then he asked if I had heard what was happening in Germany. I confessed that I had not and he went on to describe that times may be changing. He told how ECPA, the European Crop Protection Association, composed at the time of twelve agrochemical companies, had begun funding an organisation in Germany to promote something which, when translated, was Integrated Crop Management. And he thought it might be possible to persuade ECPA to supply seed funding for something similar in Britain. And he said it was aiming for exactly the kind of outcomes I had described in my Memphis speech.

"Well, you'd have to call it something different in Britain," I retorted. "Nobody will know what you're talking about." And there and then we dreamed up the name 'Linking Environment and Farming' and the acronym LEAF and I drew a LEAF shape with the letters inside it on the back of an aircraft menu.

"If I can persuade ECPA to provide some funds, would you be interested in being involved?" he said. Of course, I said yes. A few weeks later I was called to a committee meeting in London where we discussed the way forward. A few weeks after that I went to another meeting where I was made chairman and the rest, as they say, is history.

We appointed Caroline Drummond as coordinator, I travelled the country promoting our ideas and thirty years later LEAF has far exceeded my expectations. Tragically Caroline died in 2022, far too young, but her legacy is an organisation whose influence has spread round the world. And despite my initial doubts, every farmer now knows what integrated farming is all about.

America is a big country and its inhabitants speak a similar language to we Brits – two countries divided by a single language as it's been observed before. So it was not surprising that as my association with AgriTravel (later Field Farm Tours) developed, some travellers wanted to visit different regions of the States.

One memorable tour I led went to California, a state that is almost a country on its own. In fact, it produces and exports more agricultural produce than any country in the world except the Netherlands, another phenomenon which I will come to later. But the whole of California is essentially a desert so while the growth-stimulating heat occurs naturally, the moisture to germinate and fill the crops has to be added artificially.

Fortunately, just to the east of the state, lie the Rocky Mountains which are covered with snow every winter. When spring comes that snow melts and has to make its way to the sea. It does so via a series of rivers that lead across California towards the Pacific. And American technology through dams and canals has captured most of that snow melt for domestic and agricultural use. Indeed, when I stood on the bank of the San Francisco River it was little more than a trickle as it made its way to the Pacific.

Access to that water, which is made available at historically low prices, has made Californian farms highly productive, particularly of horticultural crops that are very marketable and exportable. Two crops per year on the same land, made possible by the combination of heat from the sun and irrigation, is the norm not the exception. But the amount of irrigation water used in such intensive production is commonly the equivalent of 50 to 60 inches of rain per year. For comparison, Norfolk farmers who irrigate their potatoes use about 5 to 6 inches in a dry year.

The use of such high quantities of water has, however, caused salt from the subsoil to rise to the surface on some fields where the practice has been going on for many years and that land has had to be abandoned because it will no longer grow crops. The state is big enough so that those farmers affected have just moved on to other virgin areas and started again. But our party did not think such habits could have a long-term future.

Our party had landed in Los Angeles and travelled by bus northwards. As we were approaching the town of Fresno, one of the party came forward to me at the front of the bus to say that a passenger at the back had been taken ill. I went back to investigate and sure enough he looked bad. His skin was as red as a telephone box and he was delirious. We needed a hospital, fast. I returned to the front of the bus and told the driver of the situation. And just then a police car pulled up alongside us. The driver opened the passenger door and shouted to the policeman that we needed "a medical room". "Follow me," said the cop and off we went, breaking every speed limit, until we reached a hospital.

We were scheduled to book into a hotel in town and I had responsibility for the other twenty-nine passengers so I asked Lorna, who had some nursing training, to look after the ill man while I got the rest to the hotel. I said she should get a taxi to the hotel and I would see her later. Her description of what she saw in the hospital was, to say the least, shocking. Just inside the door was a man on a gurney with blood all over him and two policemen holding him down. Further on in the queue was another policeman, this one handcuffed to another obvious criminal. Seeing the state of our fellow passenger, the receptionist beckoned him and Lorna forward where she was handed over to a doctor who told Lorna he "just luuurved the way she talked". After which he asked if the patient was insured (yes) and demanded $100 before he would even look at him. Fortunately, Lorna had kept her handbag with her and paid him. But experiences like that don't half make you appreciate the NHS.

As an aside, we stayed in a series of multistorey hotels in California and three times in two different hotels we were woken in the middle of the night by fire alarms and announcements telling us to vacate our rooms, come down the stairs (not the lifts, for obvious reasons) and gather in the street in front of the building. I did a count of our party on one of these occasions, stood there on the sidewalk in a variety of coloured pyjamas and nightdresses, and realised a few were missing. Fortunately, all the alarms were false so it didn't matter. And at breakfast the following morning those who had not been present outside admitted they had slept through the excitement.

Continuing the irrigation theme, I went for a short trip to America as a guest of Tate & Lyle. It was during the bidding war between the Italian firm, Ferruzzi, and Tate & Lyle for British Sugar, the monopoly processor of sugar beet in Britain. In the end, neither of them got it because it went to Associated British Foods who own it to this day. But both Ferruzzi and Tates thought they should own it and as *Farming Diary* was the only TV programme for farmers in the main UK growing area we were targeted for potential publicity. Ferruzzi flew a film crew to Italy, of which more later, and Tate & Lyle flew us to Denver near where they had beet processing plants.

They had, in fact, recently bought a company called Crystal Sugar which had a few factories in Colorado and Montana. They really wanted us to see the one in Billings, but Denver was the nearest international airport. So, we were driven from Denver to Billings and did most of our interviews around that factory. It was a bit ancient but it was the best one Tates had bought so it would have to do. It operated exactly like the ones in this country, the main difference was that all the beet had to be lifted and clamped by the end of October because later than that and they may be frozen in the ground. So there was an annual scramble to get the crop clamped and covered and the factory then collected the roots from clamps as they needed them.

We spoke to a number of growers to hear their views on how they had been treated by Crystal/Tates and were not surprised to hear some of the same grumbles you would hear from British growers about the then current management of the UK processor. But one of the main complaints they expressed was that they were not able to irrigate their crops which they reckoned would have increased their yields by 25% to 30%. The reason? Because "them rich folks in Denver had bought all the water rights. If you got enough money you can change the laws of nature and make water run up hill." Denver, may I remind you, is known as the mile-high city.

Another tour for AgriTravel started in Texas then Oklahoma (where the corn was as high as an elephant's eye!) and moved north through the Midwest ending in Iowa and flying home for Chicago. The TV programme *Dallas* was popular at the time and we still didn't know who had killed JR, so we decided to go to Southfork, just outside the city, home of the fictional Ewings, which was by this time open for visitors. It was surprisingly small and the swimming pool was tiny whereas it had looked quite large on the programme. Must be trick photography we decided. Inside the house, some areas were roped off so that we didn't soil any of the familiar artefacts. But Lorna was a pianist and couldn't resist stepping over one rope that protected the grand piano. She sat on the stool and proceeded to play a Scottish reel but the instrument was so far out of tune that she gave up before a guard came and removed her.

While in Texas we went to one of the legendary beef lots with animals penned in lots of a hundred or so, being fed alfalfa cut from fields all around the area and maize silage conserved in huge clamps. Most were Hereford type cattle and we had to accept that they looked in very good condition despite the lack of any bedding and the smell of their faeces that permeated the area.

"So, you like my cattle?" asked the manager. We nodded and he said, "The feed is real good and the hormones help." And he went on to tell us that they administered three doses of hormone to every animal during its stay in the lot. In other words, a dose every three months. In Britain we had banned even one dose per animal in case it affected the sex lives of the people who ate the beef. But we didn't think one or two American steaks would hurt us too much and I had to admit they tasted good and juicy.

Near Oklahoma City we visited a huge dairy unit of 12,000 cows divided into 1,000 cow lots. It was owned by a man who had flown bombing missions from Britain into Germany during the Second World War. He had survived and when he returned to America had set up a chain of milk bars. The chain had grown and his dairy unit supplied all of them. He welcomed us like old friends. He had developed an affection for our country while serving there and was proud to show us his cows.

You might expect that a unit involving 12,000 cows would be a nightmare but I can honestly say I have never seen a more immaculate set-up. Each 1,000-cow unit was built alongside the next. The cows were housed and fed at one end and milked at the other. The floor of the lying area between the cubicles was swept clean and you could eat your lunch off the surface of any item in the series of milking parlours. The cows looked well and walked well. There was a team of vets and AI men employed to ensure good health and good breeding records. In short, it was as good an example of expert husbandry as you would ever hope to see. We came away thoroughly impressed.

Northwest a bit through Yellowstone Park, which is as big as Wales by the way, taking in the Old Faithful geyser which erupts every fifty or so minutes, to Salt Lake City, Utah, home of the Mormons. I wanted to go there partly out of curiosity and partly because the Mormons had been buying farms in East Anglia and I wanted to see where they had come from. Our reception by the formally suited and highly disciplined elders who greeted us was friendly and helpful. We wanted to see and hear how these disciples of the Church of Latter-Day Saints lived and worshipped. We were taken to the huge church and invited to walk round it. When I say huge, it was bigger than any theatre I had ever been in and sloped like a giant lecture hall with pulpit and organ on a stage at the front. A choir was practising as we quietly toured the building and their sound was beautiful.

Towards the end of our tour, we were directed to a kind of lounge area where there were easy chairs and a video played on a loop. It told of Mormon beliefs supported by quotations from the Bible and ended with an invitation to learn more from the elders who hovered around us. Next we were invited to go with a couple of young people, obviously trainees, to see parcels of goods being prepared to be sent to China as a goodwill gesture.

There had just been a catastrophic earthquake in Haiti so I asked whether any parcels might be diverted there, which seemed to me more urgent. "We don't know anything about that," said one of our young guides. "But," I continued, "you must have heard about it on the news." "We're not encouraged to watch TV or listen to the news," was the response. And that was the end of that conversation.

I wanted to continue but it was clear that they had strict instructions not to engage in anything beyond *The Book of Mormon*. Furthermore, they were being shut off from what was happening in the rest of the world. We left town without being impressed by their way of life, even the habit that some of them practise of taking a handful of wives. It just didn't appeal to us men or our wives.

Our route next took us west through Wyoming and Nebraska to Iowa and the 'corn and hogs' state. We were to visit friends there at the town of Waverly. Fran and Howard Mueller had joined us on a few of these tours before having flown in from America to do so and they had become great friends. Howard was a deep-voiced grain farmer as well as acting as a government advisor in Washington. Fran was the director of the local hospital as well as serving on many other local charities. They were a charming couple and welcomed our group into their lovely house for a slap-up lunch. The opportunity to see inside people's houses and get to know them is a privilege many of our trips have provided and it is so much more informative than hotels, however many stars they boast.

After lunch, Howard gave us a tour of the local area, including the John Deere headquarters, and the next day he took us to see where he loaded barges with his grain so that it would eventually end up sailing down the Mississippi to the Gulf. Alongside the landing stage was a huge cave that you could drive a bus through – we did it – which was used as a store for harvested grain. It was perfectly dry and there were dozens of different discreet areas in the cave, each one of which was as big as a 1,000-tonne barn and traders rented what space they needed until the right barge came along. Another new and unique experience.

We were due to fly home from Chicago, Illinois, the neighbouring state to Iowa so I made contact with an old friend I had worked with in Norfolk who I knew was in Chicago at the time. His name was Stuart Garner and he had been the editor of our local paper, of which I was a non-executive director, and he had been headhunted by Thompsons Newspapers to run their North American chain of papers. He'd booked a table for he and his wife, Lorna and I at a restaurant called the Chicago Chop House, one of the top eateries in town. I remember that I had crabs' claws as a main course and I can taste them now. They were delicious.

Beef cattle ready for the auction, Kansas City

Kansas City Stock Yards

The party that went to the USA, with Winston Churchill outside the British Embassy in Washington

Lorna jumped the rope and played the piano at Southfork, Dallas Texas

The famous Fishermans Wharf, San Francisco

The Golden Gate Bridge, San Francisco

San Francisco trams

Mounted Police, Washington

The Rocky Mountains

Lorna and a giant redwood or sequoia, California

FRANCE

A year or two after I joined the BBC as a freelance broadcaster in 1962, I was asked by Anthony Parkin, the producer of *On Your Farm* on Radio 4, to go to France to cover the Paris Show. Held in twelve huge exhibition halls at Porte de Versailles, it was a bit like the Smithfield Show in London's Earls Court but much bigger. In those days in the 1960s, the show included cattle and sheep and other livestock as well as machinery together with one of my favourite halls, devoted to French food. The event has outgrown the Versailles site now and while farm machinery is still exhibited there, the livestock have apparently moved to another site near Le Bourget airport.

The show was and is one of the biggest in the world for farm equipment and every year attracted more than a million visitors over a week at the end of February and the beginning of March. One of our main reasons for attending was because the British Agricultural Exports Council had decided to exhibit in the hall devoted to foreign countries. Being absolutely honest, it was a big disappointment compared with other countries' exhibits. Countries like Germany, Italy, Spain and had massive stands promoting their national products and food. Obviously these had been generously supported by their governments and they were very impressive and well-manned.

The British offering was a series of small booths made of some sort of plywood decorated with some Union Jacks. In each booth sat one or two disconsolate representatives of British firms doing their best to drum up enthusiasm for whatever it was they were trying to sell. To say it looked like Britain was trying to do it on the cheap was an understatement.

I interviewed the then chairman of the Export Council, Rudi Sternberg, an Eastern European gentleman who had been asked by the British government to head up the organisation because he had a farm in Kent, had contacts across Europe and spoke several languages. I put it to him that the British exhibit was not up to the standard of the other nations. He replied, in broken English, that his Council had very little money because the British government was too mean to support it as other governments had. He ended our chat by saying we must do better next year and with the memorable phrase, "Vee British, vee got to schtick togezzer."

But the rest of the show was fantastic. Machines of every colour and make and some of them were huge. We've seen limited numbers of such big tackle in Britain since then but it was pointed out to me that the event attracted buyers from places like Russia, Australia, America where multi-hundred-acre fields were common and such big machines were justified. I'd been brought up to believe that we were the most efficient farmers in the world but that first time in Paris made me realise that Britain was a minor force in farming.

There were also some breeds of cattle that I'd never seen before. The Charolais had just begun to be known in Britain having been given a license to be imported a few years previously. But Limousins and Normandes and Simmentals and Chianinas from Italy, plus a few more that I was less impressed by, were all new to me and most other British farmers who were there. All of them are familiar these days since the government relaxed the rules on importation. But it would have been at shows like this that UK stockmen decided to try some new blood on their farms.

And then there was the food hall. It was packed most of the time as Frenchmen and women and people like me queued for snacks between touring the other stands. One of my favourites was croque monsieur – melted cheese on bread over ham – again new to me at the time. Another was freshly baked French bread with liver pâté. I know they force feed the geese to make their livers fat but my goodness the pâté is good. And for dessert a crepe, cooked in front of you and laced with a slug of brandy. We hadn't seen or tasted any of these delights in Britain in the 1960s and discovering them was a revelation.

We were in Paris for a few days that first time, so we needed feeding in the evenings and by accident we found a restaurant named Les Trois Limousins not far from the Champs-Élysées. The menu on the window promised Limousin steaks so we decided to find out if they tasted as good as they looked. There was a stuffed Limousin bullock in one corner and they sat us close to it. Vegetarians would not have been comfortable. But I don't suppose they would have gone into the restaurant in the first place. And the steaks were delicious.

Next morning we caught the Metro back to Porte de Versailles to do more interviews. I'm not sure how my breath smelled but most of our fellow passengers had eaten something with garlic in it and the whole carriage stank of it. When we emerged into the daylight, we were just in time to see President de Gaulle arriving at the show. His convoy of cars was surrounded by police on motorcycles and I glanced up to see rows of riflemen on top of buildings ready to react if anything untoward happened.

Suddenly de Gaulle's car stopped and out he got – a tall man in full military uniform – and headed towards the crowds on the street, hands outstretched to shake those of his waiting fans. The security detail had not expected this, despite de Gaulle being known for such gestures, and you could almost see them tighten their fingers on the triggers of their guns. Nothing happened, thank goodness, and after a few minutes of pressing the flesh he got back in his car and continued into the show. I remembered that moment when, a few years later, I read *The Day of the Jackal* by Frederick Forsyth.

I went to several Paris Shows over the years with Anthony Parkin for radio's *On Your Farm*, with BBC TV cameras for the *Farming* programme that went out on Sunday lunchtimes and later after I had left the BBC and joined Anglia TV we filmed there for *Farming Diary* which I presented. But that first visit was the most memorable simply because it was all new to me.

Anglia seemed to have a more generous budget than the BBC and the producer of *Farming Diary*, Bill Smith, was able to hire a private plane to take us to Paris. On one of these occasions we took off from Norwich in an eight-seater, twin prop aircraft with four seats either side of the fuselage and had just settled down for the two-hour flight when the cameraman, who was sitting over the right wing, turned to me sitting behind him and said, "Have you seen the oil leaking out of the engine cowling?" I looked and oil was spurting out of the top of the wing. "For God's sake, tell the pilot!" I shouted. He did and when he saw the leak I could see his neck go white as he switched off the engine and radioed to Norwich that we were coming back. He flew the plane on one engine back to where we had come from and we were met by two fire engines on the runway. Fortunately the leaky engine did not get quite hot enough to fly on fire and we got back OK on one engine. We were a little late getting to the show that year.

Anglia also sought out the best restaurants to eat and on one visit to Paris the whole crew went to a two-Michelin-star establishment called Le Taillevent. As we sat contemplating the menu, the waiter, a very supercilious individual with a long aristocratic nose, asked if we would like to order some wine. At which point Oliver Walston, my co-presenter, said, "Leave this to me" and told him that we would like two bottles of house red and two bottles of house white. To which the waiter looked down his nose and said, "All ze wine is of ze 'ouse monsieur. Which would you like?"

On another occasion I flew with an Anglia TV crew to Nevers in central France where we had heard farmers were planning to demonstrate against the local mayor. Or as someone said, "The peasants are revolting." In those days, they did it a lot and it certainly had an effect on the deal they got from their government and beyond that from the European Union.

We arrived at the point where the march was to start to find many hundreds of farmers armed with milk churns and other farm tools as weapons already getting into their stride. As they marched, creating havoc along the street, they were met by busloads of French riot police complete with batons and shields. As the farmers became even more truculent, the police began throwing tear gas at them and we were caught in the middle of it. It was the first, and last, time I have experienced tear gas and I can feel it now – an intense stinging in the eyes that no amount of covering or rubbing can relieve. It took hours for my eyes to feel normal again.

Another riot I got caught in was outside the European Parliament in Strasbourg. A debate about farm prices was going on inside the building and farmers from several European Common Market nations decided to march on the building to let their views be known about the inadequacy of the prices that had been proposed. Once again, the riot police were out to stop the rioters getting into the parliament building. I went out to get some photographs of the affair and found myself the target for stones and sticks thrown by the farmers. I tried shouting that I was one of them and wanted more from the CAP like they did. It probably didn't help that I shouted in English. Anyway, I managed to get back into the building relatively unscathed and carried on interviewing MEPs.

But not all French farmers were aggressive. At times they were very hospitable and I suffered from that too. It was when I was with the BBC and we had travelled to Britanny in the northwest corner of France to do a story about the export of cauliflowers – or *choux-fleurs* as the French call them – to southern English ports. The added interest to this was that the trade was organised by a cooperative based at Landerneau. There was a great deal of interest in farmer cooperation in the UK at the time and the Landerneau coop consisted of many very small farmers. We wanted to know how they made it work in France but UK farmers were reluctant to follow suit.

We travelled around Britanny talking to farmers, filmed their pack house and the port operation from which the cauliflowers left for England and talked to the managers of the business. They were thrilled at our interest and insisted on giving the whole film crew lunch in their boardroom. We didn't have time for such luxuries because we had a schedule to keep. But Mike Marshall, the producer, felt it would be rude to refuse after all the help they had given us and said, "OK, just a quick one." But you don't get quick lunches in France and this one lasted about three hours.

It was a Friday and the board of directors were mainly Catholics, so we were served fish. The first course was six oysters in their shells. They were so fresh that when I squeezed lemon juice on them they squiggled. I got them down somehow and hoped for a main course that was easier to swallow. It was octopus (not those little things you see in salads, real octopus) served in some kind of thick tomato sauce. I almost gagged as I tried to swallow pieces of tentacle and did not do justice to their generous hospitality. And eventually we got away, very much behind schedule. Because we were booked on a hovercraft to Jersey where we were to film another story for the programme.

On the way to the hoverport I developed a violent stomach-ache and had to be sick on the side of the road. But I had to record a piece to camera to introduce the cauliflower film and it had to be done in the Brittany countryside. We found a suitable spot and I did my introduction. It wasn't wonderful because I was still suffering and it showed on the film. But it had to do and we proceeded to the hovercraft. If you have ever been on one you will know that they can be bumpy and on this evening the sea was rough. It was the most uncomfortable ride I have ever had. And when we arrived at our Jersey hotel I went straight to bed and slept for twelve hours because of the pain I'd been through. The things I did for the BBC!

On another occasion I drove to France in my Rover car to record a continental breakfast. Older readers might remember that Anthony Parkin and I often interviewed notable people across their breakfast table. The programmes went out on Saturday mornings at 7.15 and Anthony reasoned that if the recording was done at about the same time it would add realism and credibility to the broadcast. And we really did eat breakfast with our subjects as we recorded them.

On this occasion we had driven down into central France to interview a Charolais breeder across his breakfast table. We ate croissants and French bread, not bacon and egg like we would have done at home. The recording completed, we set off in my car heading for Paris. We had arranged to interview somebody in Belgium later that day and we had to go by Paris.

It was a hot July day and as we reached the Paris ring road – or *peripherique* – the car began to splutter. I knew immediately what was wrong. It was a good car and went well 99% of the time but in hot weather, particularly in slow traffic, the petrol had a habit of volatilising in the carburettor. It was easily corrected. I had to raise the bonnet, unscrew the top of the carburettor and pour a little petrol in it. Then screw it back together again, close the bonnet and away it would go. But imagine doing that on the *peripherique*.

There were four lanes of traffic and I had to find my way to the slowest lane with a spluttering engine. Anthony began to panic because he didn't know what was happening as I changed lanes and stopped. Behind me cars started to hoot their horns but I couldn't help it. I asked Anthony to get out and direct the cars around mine while I got my spanners and little bottle of petrol I kept in the boot for such occasions. It didn't take long but, with all the horns blaring and the embarrassment, it seemed ages. We got back in the car and all was well. But I sold that car soon after that incident. A pity because in cool weather it was a very good vehicle indeed.

I can't finish this chapter on France without recalling a visit I arranged to Paris to celebrate Lorna's and my fifth wedding anniversary. We'd had a very modest honeymoon in London and had to return home a couple of days earlier than planned because we ran out of money. So, when I started earning a bit from broadcasting I felt I owed her a bit of a treat. I booked a place for my car on the ferry from Dover to Calais and we set off.

All went well until we joined the autoroute to Paris. I suddenly had to hold onto the steering wheel while travelling at about 80kms per hour. I managed to get to the side of the road, got out to investigate and sure enough, we had a front wheel puncture. I got the spare wheel and the jack out of the boot while Lorna tried to direct traffic around me. The puncture was on the left side of the car beside the traffic, so it was a rather dangerous situation. Finally, I got the spare fitted and the punctured tyre in the boot and we set off again, wondering where I would get the puncture mended.

When we got to Paris we had to find somewhere to stay. I had not pre-booked anywhere because I was sure we could find a moderately priced place when we got there. And after driving round a series of side streets we did just that. It was a four-storey hotel with a madame in charge who escorted us to a top-floor room. It had an ensuite bathroom complete with bidet and a double bed. The hotel did not serve *petit dejeuner* – breakfast – but we could easily get a croissant and a coffee at a nearby cafe, so no problem. It was plain but within my budget and we took it for three nights – payment upfront.

The room was reasonably comfortable but there seemed to be a lot of activity up and down the stairs. This went on through the late evening and into the night and disturbed our sleep somewhat. It was only when I heard the unmistaken sound of bouncing bed springs in the next room that I began to realise we had inadvertently booked ourselves into a house of ill repute. The activity on the stairs and the opening and shutting of doors was ladies of the night bringing their clients in and out of the bedrooms. But we'd booked for three nights and paid upfront so we stuck it out.

During the few days we were in Paris we did lots of touristy things that my previous trips to cover the Paris Show had not allowed. We went up the Eiffel Tower, we visited the Palace of Versailles, took a boat trip on the Seine and so on as well as finding a garage to mend the puncture. And on our last evening I took Lorna to see the show at the Moulin Rouge. To be honest I rather wanted to see it myself. Before the show we went to a little restaurant near the theatre for an early dinner. I had some pâté as a starter which I did not enjoy. In fact I thought it was off and didn't finish it. Lorna, thankfully, had something else.

After dinner we walked to the Red Mill – Moulin Rouge – and took our seats high up in the gallery (the only tickets I could afford). The show began and the famous dancing girls with legs about six feet long and wearing a few ostrich feathers and not much else began going through their routine. And at that point the pâté got me. I had to push past other theatre goers and race to the lavatory where I sat for most of the first half of the programme. I resumed my seat for the second half but the pâté got me again and it was a repeat performance through the second act. Lorna said it was a good show and that she had enjoyed it. I couldn't comment because I'd spent most of the time in the loo.

We returned to our hotel, had another disturbed night, found our car, and drove back to Calais, the ferry and home, without incident. I was quite pleased to be home!

BELGIUM

When Britain first joined the Common Market (that's what it was called before it became the EU) farm prices were negotiated by the then ten member nations in much the same way we had been used to in Britain. In other words, each farm commodity was considered separately and the price paid to farmers for the coming year agreed. It wasn't quite as easy as that of course because each country had its priorities, and they were different to those of other countries. Italy wanted the best deal it could get for olive oil, France fought for sugar beet, Holland for potatoes and so on.

So, every February or March the agriculture ministers of each nation would gather in Brussels and meet in the magnificent Berlaymont building to try to thrash out some deals. The ministers met around a big table on the thirteenth floor and the press corps, of which I was often a member, crowded into a much smaller room on the ground floor. The negotiations would usually begin on a Monday with each minister and his or her hangers-on (advisors!) arriving in some style in chauffeur-driven black Mercedes cars. The press would shout questions at them in multiple languages asking them about their forthcoming stance on this or that commodity, receiving no answers, and the ministers would proceed through the throng with enigmatic smiles.

The negotiations were usually scheduled to last about three days. But that was an optimistic guess because they always ran over time, frequently into the following weekend. And that was despite late-night sittings with us hacks sitting drinking coffee out of polystyrene cups to stay awake. Every now and then an advisor to one or other of the delegations would come down and whisper unattributable information to the reporters from his nation and they would then scurry into the typewriter room to file copy to their newsrooms about "rumours" reflecting what they had just been told.

It was the most boring job I ever did for the BBC because it was only when there was a final agreement that I, as the interviewer, could speak to our minister and record, or film, something for our TV programme. But there was one occasion when the negotiations had been particularly difficult and long-winded when we had a brief break from the smoke-filled press room. Henry Plumb, who was president of the National Farmers Union at the time, came into the press room to see if he could check on progress. It was Friday evening at about eleven o'clock and somehow the fact that he was there became known upstairs. Fred Peart, who was the UK minister of agriculture, sent a message that the British press contingent were invited upstairs for a drink. So, into the lift and up we went to the thirteenth floor.

Each countries' delegation had its own office around the negotiating room and we, and Henry Plumb (who I knew well), were ushered into the British office which was surprisingly spacious. Fred Peart, who liked a glass or two, was holding court and when he saw Henry and our group he staggered over, drink in hand, and said in his Cumbrian accent, "I expect you lads would like to see a scrap between Henry and me. What a good story that would make. Well, I'm not going to fight him", and here he paused to put his arm round Henry's shoulder and went on, "Because we're good friends, aren't we Henry?" To which Henry reluctantly agreed to hide his embarrassment.

I wasn't too surprised at Peart's behaviour. I'd witnessed it before in Broadcasting House in London when he had refused to do an interview for radio until he'd consumed almost a bottle of wine in the Green Room. The interview wasn't very good for obvious reasons. But here he was, in charge of negotiating a deal that would affect the livelihoods of British farmers and he could hardly stand. Thank goodness for Freddie Kearns the Permanent Secretary and MAAF at the time. He was as sharp as a tack and in reality was doing most of the negotiating. Indeed, it was said that Peart had spent the last two evenings playing snooker in a Brussels bar while Kearns argued Britain's case around the table.

But Kearns had his weak spots too. When one of the journalists asked him if he thought the negotiations would be finished that night, he replied, "If it's down to me they will be. In fact, one of my chaps said to me just now that he thought we might be here all weekend. I was so angry I punched him in the guts. I apologised later because one shouldn't treat civil servants like that. But I'm determined to get to the game at Twickenham tomorrow afternoon." Everything was agreed a couple of hours later.

But at the beginning of those weeks of negotiations we knew there was no point in hanging around the press room because the delegations would still be putting their case to one another and the European officials whose job it was to supervise a deal within budget, and no agreement was likely. So we sought out some of the fine restaurants off the central square where the little boy pees into a pond (it's a statue by the way, in case you were wondering). There I was introduced to my first plate of mussels for which Brussels is famous. You finish up with as big a pile of shells as you had to start with but the mussels you've dug out of them are delicious.

Some years later after Henry Plumb had served his term as president of the NFU and gone on to be elected to the European Parliament which in turn elected him its president, he asked me to help him organise a world farming and food conference. Held in Brussels under the auspices of the European Parliament, it attracted delegates from around the world. Henry had made many contacts during his time in agri politics and this was his time to call in some favours. One of the most colourful people who attended was Jomo Kenyatta, president of Kenya.

Henry had known him for some years and I'm not sure whether he had invited him to speak at the pre-conference dinner but he did anyway. He was accompanied by a soldier in full dress uniform and medals and when Kenyatta decided to speak this soldier marched behind him and produced his speech from a folder with a great flourish. Kenyatta delivered it without looking at it – it was very much an off-the-cuff performance – and then proceeded to sing to the assembled company. He had a deep baritone voice but I think the words were in the Kikuyu language so I have no idea what it was about. Eventually he left the podium and the evening continued as already planned.

The conference went well, with speakers emphasising, even then in 1988, the future vulnerability of world food supplies to increasing population, reducing freshwater availability and civil unrest. But as so many times since, I'm not sure any of the politicians who could make a difference were listening.

But agriculturalists and scientists were doing their best to bridge that potential gap. One of them was Professor Laloux, one of the authors of the mini revolution in wheat growing of the 1980s. At the time there were two main sources of data for farmers to follow. One was from researchers in Schleswig-Holstein in northern Germany and the other was from Laloux's Belgian university. Both came about from research showing that yields of wheat, in particular, could be enhanced by spraying sulphur on them at critical times to help control leaf disease. Combined with splitting nitrogen top dressings into three applications through the growing season, rather than one at the beginning of spring, this had a dramatic effect and as sprays became more sophisticated yields were even better.

Clearly this technique was of interest to the viewers of *Farming Diary* which I was presenting for Anglia TV so a visit to Belgium was called for. I was particularly keen to learn about it myself as a wheat grower and because I had predicted what was about to happen at a conference in Bournemouth arranged by the *Power Farming* magazine. I had been studying the emergence of the research and suggested to the conference that in order to capitalise on the coming system it would be necessary to develop integrated systems of drilling, spraying and fertilising that used the same wheel ways through the crop – like *tramlines,* I said. The press picked up on my description and today every arable farmer in Britain uses tramlines on every field of cereals.

During another visit to Brussels to report on some debate or other I was in the Parliament building there. I should remind readers that the European Parliament met some of the time in Strasbourg and some of the time in Brussels. And this was the turn of Brussels. Henry Plumb was in charge, of course, and invited me to have lunch with him in the 'canteen' or as I would describe it, the 'five-star restaurant' for MEPs. I accepted, of course, and was somewhat perplexed when Henry sat me next to the Reverend Ian Paisley who was an MEP for Northern Ireland. I had seen him on TV news bulletins raving about Papists and Republicans on his home turf but didn't know what to expect over lunch. Suffice to say he was charming. He knew a lot about farming but was prepared to listen to my opinion as well, and he didn't rave at me once. We parted good friends and Henry winked at me and said, "You didn't expect that, did you?"

Much later, after I had helped to found LEAF (Linking Environment and Farming) in the early 1990s, I was invited to speak at a conference in Brussels promoting Integrated

Farm Management. Sponsored by the European Parliament itself, it was intended to help educate MEPs and EU officials about the farming system which advocated care for the environment alongside the production of affordable food. It was probably the most high-profile audience I had ever addressed and I hope it did a little to convince them of the importance of agriculture as they attempted to manage the, by then, twenty-seven member states. Except now there are only twenty-six since Britain voted to leave.

I am convinced that was one of the biggest mistakes we have ever made and the difficulties of exporting goods to Europe together with higher costs of almost everything surely prove it. It seemed to me then, as it still does, that this is the time to join forces with friendly nations, not split from them. The EU was not and is not perfect. But surely it would have been better to try to make it better from within, not leave and risk hostility from them. Brexit enthusiasts thought they would be able to forget regulations and that British politicians would be better than 'unelected' Brussels bureaucrats and did not realise that some of our *elected* bureaucrats and politicians are far worse. But what is done is done and I don't suppose we will ever re-join the EU.

CHINA

The phone rang and it was an old friend from Young Farmers Club days, Jill Lewis, who was now running a farmers travel firm called the Agricultural Travel Bureau. She'd started in the travel business with another old friend called Bob Martin who had previously been a County Organiser for Young Farmers. Bob had retired and Jill took over the business. Her call was to ask if I would like to lead a party of farmers to look at Chinese agriculture and Lorna could come too. How could I refuse?

Another old friend called Hew Watt had taken a couple of parties there for Jill previously and I had heard him enthusing about it. But he didn't want to take more and Jill had thought of me as a replacement. She told me she thought my writing and TV appearances might help attract a few people and that Hew Watt was keen to pass on what he'd learned to help us. Lorna was pleased that she might be able to join the party and Jill said she should come too to make sure I didn't make a fool of myself. All we had to do was persuade people to book to travel with us.

It was 1980 and there was a great deal in the news about the changes in China. Mao Zedong had died in 1976 to be replaced, briefly, by the Gang of Four which included Mao's widow. But their ruthless regime was short-lived and Deng Xiaoping was installed as the new president. One of his first acts was to decree that couples could only have one child because the Chinese population was increasing too fast. He was also planning to open up the Chinese economy, it was reported.

With all these things in the news there was a lot of interest in China and we soon had thirty people wanting to come with us. So, in September the following year – 1981 – we set off for Beijing. In those days aircraft didn't fly far on one fill-up of fuel so we stopped to refuel in Rome, Dubai, Delhi and Hong Kong. We arrived a few hours later than scheduled in Beijing, twenty-eight hours after taking off in London. Needless to say, we were shattered and a bit grumpy when we met our guide at Beijing airport, especially when she told us to hurry because we were late. It turned out we had been booked to attend a performance of traditional Chinese music at a theatre in town and she expected us to be there no matter the length of our journey.

About half of the party said they would not go to the performance and went straight to bed once we reached our government guest house. But the other half of us gave in to the guide's bullying and went along. What we had not realised was that as honoured guests we had seats on the front row of the stalls. As the plinkity-plonkity music, which I am sure was wonderful to Chinese ears, continued I'm afraid I dozed off time and time again. What the musicians thought of us I can't imagine. But perhaps they didn't care because during the interval I asked our guide why so many people behind us were talking during the concert. "Why shouldn't they talk if they want to?" she retorted. "They are as good as the people on the stage."

Fortunately the tourist system in China at the time decreed that when we moved from place to place the guides changed and the rest of them were much nicer than the one in Beijing. But while we were there, she told us that there were nine million bicycles in Beijing. And we believed her, for the streets were filled with them carrying incredible loads that included live chickens, pigs and other animals for them to eat; crates full of vegetables; goods of every shape and size; passengers front and back and everything else you could imagine. And every now and then a big black car with smoky windows would come by, scattering all before it. "That will be a government minister," our guide would say, with no rancour despite her obviously Communistic views.

Everyone was dressed in Mao-style navy suits – men and women. There seemed no difference so far as uniform was concerned and certainly no attempt by the women to glam up. The only difference was with the children. The one child per family rule was already showing itself and those couples with a young child were clearly trying to make their offspring as smart as possible. We looked at them and wondered how they would grow up after such pampering and being spoiled.

Our hotel, as I have already alluded to, was a guest house run by the government. It was spacious, comfortable and ensuite but there was no kettle for tea making. Instead, a little woman brought a flask of hot water and green tea leaves. I had bought a new toothbrush for the trip but foolishly had not thrown out my old one, so disposed of it in the waste bin in the bathroom. Four days later my old toothbrush caught up with me. The maid had found it and presumably thought I had dropped it accidentally and sent it forward to the next place we were staying.

We visited the Forbidden City, a palace used by emperors that was full of historic artefacts. We went to Tiananmen Square next to the Great Hall of the People, where my friend Kate Adie of BBC News nearly got shot in 1989 as she was reporting the army putting down the uprising when Deng feared his reforms had gone too far. We took a bus trip to the Great Wall and climbed up a steep slope on it to one of the lookout posts. When we came down some of the ladies needed the loo. As always with ladies, they had to queue and when they returned to the bus some were laughing, others were disgusted. Apparently the loo consisted of a dwarf wall on which they had to wait for a space to become available to sit and behind it was an open sewer.

We were all very pleased that the following day we were to leave the Beijing area and travel out into the countryside and visit some farms. On the way we visited what I can only describe as a series of allotments growing vegetables intended for the Beijing market. They looked extremely healthy and our guide explained that they were being fertilised organically. Further questioning revealed that the fertiliser was human sewage mixed with water and spread on the crops through buckets with holes in the bottom dangling from men's shoulder harnesses as they walked along the rows. We were told there were over a hundred different sorts of vegetables being grown in China and they were all available in the markets. Our party was a little less enthusiastic about eating vegetables after that visit.

The difference between the capital city and the countryside was dramatic. There were still people riding bicycles carrying impossible loads but almost the only other traffic on the roads were occasional seven-tonne lorries carrying goods into Beijing. The farms were nearly all cooperatives and state-controlled and some of them were quite extensive. But the work was being done by men and women with a few oxen and donkeys.

Whenever we arrived at a farm – and we visited several – our party was taken to a meeting room and sat down with cups of green tea. To my way of thinking it was tasteless stuff but I'm told it's become popular in Britain in recent years so I had better not criticise it. In some of the better-off communes there were paintings, or probably copies of paintings, of the Great Leader, Mao Zedong, setting off on his revolutionary march towards Communism which we were able to study. The leader of the cooperative would then come and speak to us. Often it was a woman and they would start their presentation in almost the same words (translated to us by our current guide) at every farm we visited.

"At this cooperative we produce [it varied from maize through vegetables, bananas, potatoes, tea and even fish]. We have x adults and y children. In our community we have five television sets and seven sofas. We have made much progress in increasing our production over the last few years but there is still a lot to do." OK, the number of TV sets and sofas varied but the format was always the same, clearly scripted by someone in Beijing.

Once we had finished our green tea we would then be invited to go outside to see what was being produced and where the people lived. We were shown inside people's houses, or perhaps hovels would be a better description, whether they had given permission or not, and saw what few possessions they had. We saw their beds – narrow brick-built shelves against a wall with gaps under them so they could light a fire in winter. As good as an electric blanket, I suppose, but I didn't fancy trying to sleep on the bare brickwork. At one commune we visited the people lived in caves. We went in them too and were surprised to see TV sets in some of them with receiving dishes screwed to the rock face above the doors. It made us realise the significance of how many TV sets the commune possessed as well as sofas.

We went into schools to see how the infants were being educated and in one class the children sang us a song in English. They had clearly learned it in anticipation of our visit. It was quite touching and their discipline appeared to be very strict. At another commune we went into a doctor's surgery while patients were being seen. Frankly it was embarrassing to be in a consulting room while a doctor was treating a patient. It was all traditional treatment like acupuncture and manipulation. One woman who had a bad knee had a needle inserted into it with a piece of tow fixed to the needle and set alight. We didn't wait to see how hot the needle became. But the patients seemed to take our presence in their stride. In a country with 1.4 billion people, I don't suppose they get much privacy.

Out on the farms we got close up to the work being done. Hardly any mechanisation was used, it was all hand work. I saw one farmer harrowing in some seeds. He had an ox on one trace and his wife on the other. But mainly it was big gangs of men and women hoeing or reaping or flood irrigating, guiding the water from one furrow to the next with hand hoes. It was a bit like I remembered farming at home in my early childhood, only much more so. And the women worked alongside the men apparently as equals.

There was one commune where they had just harvested their maize cobs. To dry them they scattered them across any dry piece of flat ground, or road that was handy, or tied them onto posts to complete the drying of the grains. The amount of hand work in all this was a revelation and we wondered how long the people would put up with it once they had seen on their shared TV sets what was possible in other countries.

And we went to a tea plantation where the pickers, mainly women this time, picked leaves off bushes and collected them in wicker baskets hung around their necks before taking them to a building, a bit like an oast house, for drying and further processing. It was called Dragon Well Green Tea and we all had to drink several cups of it while we listened to the usual spiel about how much they had achieved.

But some communes had diversified into higher value products like carpets, fabrics and silk for Western markets and one was specialising in carving ivory. The ivory business was still legal in the UK at the time and it was the most labour-intensive and skilled business we saw. Apparently it could take a year to carve an elephant's trunk and the end product was a thing of beauty. Not politically correct these days, of course, but true, nevertheless. And the output was clearly aimed at the tourist market. People like us, although I don't think any of our party bought any carvings. But some of the ladies were tempted by the fabrics and silks and I found a few yards of silk in our luggage when we got home.

One of the most fascinating places we visited was the tomb of the Emperor Qin Shi Huang who ruled China 2,250 years ago and the Terracotta Warriors buried with him to guard him in immortality. We had to fly to Xian several hundred miles to the west of Beijing where they had been discovered by accident by a farmer ploughing his land. The discovery had only taken place in 1976 and it was claimed at the time the greatest archaeological find of the 20th century.

By the time we visited, a huge, curved roof had been erected over the site and we were able to walk round it to see the incredible spectacle. The life-sized warriors, made of terracotta and each one different from its neighbour, were lined up in rows of four abreast as if marching. They carried different weapons, some led terracotta horses and there were hundreds of them. It was difficult to believe that the craftsmanship to produce such figures existed more than two hundred years before Christ.

Our bus had pulled up to the entrance of the building in which the warriors were now housed in the middle of a maize field. When I went back there with another party in 1999 – eighteen years later – it was all changed. The bus had to park several hundred yards from the entrance and visitors had to run the gauntlet of dozens of stalls selling a variety of bric-a-brac rubbish including mini plastic warriors. The excavations had uncovered many more warriors and there were now about 800 of them, we were told, and there could be many more as yet undiscovered. But that first time I was able to walk into the maize and photograph a lady picking cobs for her supper. My photographic session didn't last long, however. A soldier with a rifle urged me out of there pretty quickly. He didn't actually threaten me with his gun but I got the feeling he was prepared to use it if I didn't comply with his grunted instructions. Obviously I was not allowed contact with unauthorised persons. I complied.

It made me aware that we were being watched; that although we might have assumed we were free to go where we wanted, if we stepped out of line we would be stopped. An illustration of this was the motorbike rider who followed us wherever we went. He never spoke to us and never interfered with our progress. But he knew our pre-arranged programme and whichever guide we had could not change it. On the one occasion when Jill and I insisted on a change from a tourist visit to an agricultural one it took hours to get it approved by the local commissars. Another example of this was when we were staying in a hotel in the countryside and we were locked in for the night by a big gate and a padlock. There was nowhere to go anyway but by such examples we were aware we were in a police state.

Back in the east of the country again we went to Shanghai. It was by far the most emancipated city we had visited, with the occasional mini skyscraper and the bustling atmosphere of a major trading centre. A few ladies even wore coloured clothes rather than the ubiquitous Mao blue suit. We booked into a nice hotel in the main street not far from the Bund, the famous waterfront of the Huangpu River and port. After we had settled in, I decided to walk to the Bund to photograph the port. I leaned on the wall to ensure I didn't shake my camera and waited for two ships to pass one another to get a good shot.

Picture taken, I turned around to return to the hotel only to find myself surrounded by about a dozen young people. One young man, clearly their leader, said, "Herro, do you speak in the street?" I replied that I didn't mind and he continued, "Are you American?" I told him no, that I was British. "Ah so …" he went on "… what is your plofession?" I replied that I was a farmer but that I was an individual farmer, not in a commune like we had seen in China. "So, you have a big house?" I told him I had a family house. "How many servants do you have?" I told him none but said I would like to ask him a question. "Why are you asking me all these personal questions?" And he told me, "We are students at Shanghai University and our professor has told us to ask these questions of any foreigners we can find." I thanked them and they parted and allowed me to return to the hotel. But it gave me an insight as to how those students and their professor viewed the Western world.

We ended that trip in Hong Kong and spent a few days there. This was civilisation as we knew it and as I walked into the restaurant in our hotel there, I suddenly had a craving for a steak. We'd been eating meals that consisted mainly of vegetables and greens for two weeks and it did not suit me. The steak that I had tasted wonderful and it reinforced my belief that I could not become a vegetarian. I also had a suit made overnight, and it is still hanging in my wardrobe. I don't wear it these days because it must have shrunk. Or perhaps my belly has expanded.

As already indicated, I took another party to China in 1999 and the capitalist policy reforms Deng Xiaoping had introduced had had a dramatic effect. He had died in 1997 but his legacy lived on. In 1999, Beijing no longer had nine million bicycles but it seemed to have nearly as many cars that now dominated the roads and made biking hazardous. But my lasting memory that summed up that trip was of a man on his heavily loaded bike waiting at traffic lights while speaking on his mobile phone. And the smog! At times you could hardly see across the road and most people wore masks. The growth in the number of cars was partly to blame and also the coal-fired power stations which, we were told at the time, were being opened at the rate of one per week.

Traditional Chinese critics that we met called it westernisation and didn't like it at all. And it was hard to disagree. A Kentucky Fried Chicken restaurant had opened in Beijing a few years previously followed soon after by a McDonald's. Both were among the most popular eating places for young Chinese. Office blocks and multistorey flats had begun to replace the hovels that were there before and city people were looking and behaving like they do in capital cities all over the Western world. The Mao dress code had almost disappeared and men were wearing business suits and ladies the female equivalent. It seemed almost like a different country.

The old guest houses that we stayed in on our first trip had disappeared. This time we stayed in well-appointed hotels with all the conveniences you would expect in the West. We saw no sign of the motorbike man but if he was there we didn't see him. We were still expected to eat with chopsticks although knives and forks were available if requested. The food was still based on vegetables and greens with a few meat dishes, except one evening in Guangzhou, or Canton as we know it, where we were scheduled to have a dinner of festival food. Knowing that most Chinese restaurants in Britain are said to be based on Cantonese food, we were looking forward to dishes with which we might be familiar.

But first our enthusiastic guide took us to a food market. There we saw dogs, cats, rats, terrapins, various songbirds, and many other tasty offerings caged up and ready for sale, alive, to the local populace. One of the reasons for selling such things alive was that few people had refrigerators so they preferred to take them home and kill and prepare them themselves. Some of the ladies in the party were distressed to see what we would regard as pets caged and ready for slaughter. I was pretty disgusted myself.

That evening, we went into the restaurant and Lorna looked at a little pond beside the door. "Oh, look," she said, "there's something swimming in the water." "Yes," said our guide, "they're snakes and they are our first course." Lorna decided to have the alternate starter and chose a bird dish. She tried it and said it tasted good but then got a load of bones caught between her teeth. It turned out she had been eating something like a sparrow and the bones were the bird's ribs and wings.

I tried to excuse us all to our guide, who was tucking into everything, by explaining that in our culture we treated some of the dishes on offer as pets or rodents and that eating them was foreign to our instincts. "But they are delicious," she said. "You must try them." Just then, what looked like the main course came out – a suckling pig on a big platter. This looks better, we thought. Then the waiter lifted a little square of crackling from its back and placed one piece on each person's plate. He then lifted the plate and took the main body of the pig back into the kitchen. So much for festival food in Canton. It's not a bit like what you get from your local Chinese.

Food choices apart, all the cities we visited were thriving and becoming very westernised. But out in the countryside things were still virtually the same. Farmers still ploughed with oxen; they still worked in communes, although they did not repeat the same lectures as they had nineteen years previously. Otherwise not much had changed. The cities were roaring ahead economically but the countryside was being left behind. And it is important to realise that the rural population accounted for about half the population of China. It could be a recipe for another revolution, we thought, although there was no sign of another Mao Zedong to lead it.

My third trip to China was in 2008, the year the Olympics were held in Beijing. As we entered the city from the newly built airport, I could hardly believe what had been done to it in the nine years since I had been there. There were six-lane highways in and around the city; there were true skyscrapers where there had been hovels; and the area around the 'bird's nest' Olympic stadium had been completely rebuilt.

There were still a few bicycles but they were outnumbered by the Chinese-built cars, manufactured on license from European and American motor companies. If you didn't know what to look for you wouldn't know the difference from cars in the West. We went through several airports on this trip and they were all new, all beautifully designed and immaculately clean. What's more, when you alighted from your flight and made the short walk into the terminal your case was there waiting for you.

The hotels we stayed in were top class at, or above, Western standards and the service in them was professional and friendly. The dress code in the cities had gone up another notch and walking through the business centre of Beijing you would hardly know the difference from London or New York. The speed at which Chinese city people had adopted Western ways and behaviour was incredible to see.

But the rural scene was still very much the same as it had been in 1981. There were a few small combine harvesters, but the ones we saw were still using sacks to collect the grain which had to be manhandled into trailers from the ground. And most farm work continued to be done by hand. The rural population had reduced a bit but nearly half of China's people still live and work on the land. It seemed to our party that they must enjoy it rather than city life. But maybe we were wrong.

On this trip we treated ourselves to a cruise down the Yangtze River for a few days. Damming it was a project that had been talked about for a hundred years so that water could be piped north to Beijing and beyond which is a dry area. And finally in 1994 it was started and the work took seventeen years. In fact, it wasn't quite finished when we were there. The result is what is claimed to be the biggest concrete dam in the world which combines holding up the water in the river with a hydroelectric scheme. The dam, known as the Three Gorges Dam, is a mile long and raises the level of the river more than a hundred metres. Upstream, a lot of land was flooded and 1.3 million people had to be accommodated elsewhere. How awful, we thought, that all these people had been driven from their homes. And we were taken to see some of them, now housed in multistorey flats.

We sympathised with them but they were thrilled at their new homes. They had central heating and hot and cold running water – conveniences they had never had before. "But do you like multistorey life?" we asked them. "Of course," they replied. "There are lifts to carry us up and down." "And where do you work now that you are not on the land?" we enquired. "That's good too," they replied. "The government has built several factories in the area and we work there. And it's under cover and warm. Much better than working in all weathers on the farm." In other words, their standards are very different from ours and we had to accept that.

Thinking about all this, I could see that in a totalitarian state if you want to build a new airport or a skyscraper you bulldoze what was there and build it. There are no enquiries and appeals that take years. You just do it. Similarly, there is no shortage of labour. If you need a thousand men to build something you just draft them to the job. If you want to build a dam that displaces 1.3 million people, you displace them and provide alternative housing and employment.

I remembered too how the ancient Chinese had created all those terracotta warriors in or around 220 BC indicating that skills and adaptability have been in Chinese DNA for countless years. And think of all those containers that sail into Felixstowe docks full of things made in China. We were often reminded that the Chinese regard history very differently from us. To them, a hundred years is nothing in the span of human existence. Eons ago China was the most powerful nation in the world. And many Chinese believe it will be again.

One of our guides

Riding to work on his water buffalo

Picking tea leaves

Picking tea leaves

Leading his ewe to the slaughter

Chinese leisure boat. A rare sight

A local pig - it even looks Chinese

The author "supervising" work on a farm

Next page: There were nine million bicycles in Beijing

Lady receiving traditional treatment for a sore knee in a doctors surgery. Note the burning rags on the acupuncture needles

The Great Wall

You can carry anything on a bike

The Forbidden City

RUSSIA AND UKRAINE

It was 1990 and things were happening in the Soviet Union. The old guard in Moscow had collapsed and Mikhail Gorbachev was now president. He brought a brief breath of fresh air to a situation that had been the preoccupation of Western governments for decades. He spoke of glasnost and perestroika – openness and restructuring – and some in the West thought this was the end of the Cold War and that we need not worry about the threat of conflict with the USSR ever again. In passing, I should mention that Vladimir Putin was just a young man in St Petersburg, or Leningrad as it was called at the time, and no one foresaw his rule of what became the Russian Federation.

It seemed to me that it was time to visit Russia to see what was happening and I told Jill Lewis that I would like to lead a party there. She did some research and discovered that the only way to arrange a trip was through Intourist, the official tourist channel, and that would mean visits to museums and art galleries but no farms. We both agreed that this would not do and after pressurising her contacts at Intourist they reluctantly agreed that we could talk to representatives at their trade centre in Highgate – where, by coincidence, Karl Marx is buried in the cemetery. We met in London and made our way to the trade centre.

The experience was a bit like I imagined it would be in the old Soviet Union. Our credentials were checked three times by guards who didn't appear to think we should be there, and we were finally taken to an austere room to meet the man in charge of travel. He regarded us with suspicion. Gorbachev's message about openness had clearly not yet reached him. "Why do you want to visit our farms?" he asked, and, "What will you do with the information you learn?"

Eventually we convinced him that our intentions were honourable and that we were not an agricultural branch of MI6. He referred us back to the tourist office saying he would instruct them to cooperate. Jill managed to agree a programme with them that included

Moscow, St Petersburg, the Ukraine (then part of the Soviet Union) and Moldova (also part of the USSR) and included a few farms as well as some tourist destinations and we advertised the trip. Like me, many other farmers were keen to know what was going on over there and we soon filled the tour. And Jill decided she would come with us.

I was surprised that the flight from Heathrow to Moscow took only four hours. I was equally surprised when I saw that the duty free shops at Sheremetyevo airport were all Irish. We were bussed into Moscow and booked in at a huge hotel which must have had over a thousand rooms. I checked behind the pictures on the walls for bugs – negative – and we went down to dinner. The food was plain and unexciting but edible and the ice cream was excellent.

While in Moscow we took in the Kremlin with its museum, complete with the gold coaches that it was implied used to be the transport of the deposed czars. They were, of course, only for ceremonial use. I had not appreciated that inside the Kremlin walls there are five cathedrals and outside in Red Square is St Basil's with its colourful domes. We were told that "he who rules the Kremlin rules Russia". One evening we went to see a ballet in the huge hall used for Soviet Party meetings. And some of us went to a three-ring circus outside the city in the biggest big top I had ever seen.

Then a train journey, overnight, to St Petersburg. We had cabins reserved with four bunk beds in each – two up and two down. Our party then had to decide who would like to sleep with whom. Lorna and I held back and the only couple left was an elderly pair who had kept themselves to themselves on the trip so far. We settled all the others into their cabins and then went to ours where our sleeping partners had already gone to bed. The man said, "I hope you don't mind but my wife gets claustrophobic unless she has a window open so I have opened it a bit." Lorna and I were not too happy because the weather was chilly and we anticipated the open window would destroy our sleep because the train would be noisy. Then he said, "I should also tell you that my wife is suffering from diarrhoea so she will probably have to get up a few times during the night and go out to the toilet."

Suffice to say he was right and we got very little sleep on that journey. Especially when, at about 3.30am and from different bunk levels, they decided to have a conversation loud enough for each of them to hear. And we could hear them too, of course. As well as our noisy neighbours, we were a little worried about the train. It seemed to be going over potholes, which was ridiculous, but the line was certainly unlevel to the point where we wondered if the train would derail. It didn't and we arrived in St Petersburg safely, if tired. Most of the rest of the party had slept reasonably well, I think, so we tried not to let them know of our problems. But it was difficult to stay awake.

St Petersburg is a beautiful city. Not for nothing is it known as the Venice of the North. And one of the most iconic buildings there is the Summer Palace where the czars used to spend their holidays. These days it's an art gallery displaying the paintings the czar and czarina and their ancestors collected during their rule. The place is full of fantastic paintings by all the famous artists you can think of. And that first time in 1991 (yes, I've been there a second time – more later) the security was almost non-existent. There were two paintings by Leonardo da Vinci, for instance, worth millions, and beside them sat an old woman – a babushka – with an apron and a headscarf. By my second visit, about fifteen years later, following demonstrators worldwide splashing stuff over paintings and cutting them with knives, they had been covered with unbreakable glass and there was a man with a rifle nearby. A sad commentary on how society has developed.

We had with us a friend and colleague of mine, the late David Chance, who had preceded me as chairman of Loddon Farmers. David had served in the Navy during the Second World War on one of the battleships that helped aid and food to reach St Petersburg via the Baltic during Hitler's 900-day land blockade. Indeed, he had a Russian medal to prove it and he spoke a bit of Russian as well. David was travelling alone and was sharing a double room with another Norfolk farmer, Billy Hammond, a noted steam engine and old tractor enthusiast. One evening very late, David knocked on my hotel door and when I answered it he said he was sorry to disturb me but Billy had gone missing. Apparently he had disappeared after dinner and had not been seen since. What should he do? I advised him to go back to his room and go to sleep; that there was nothing we could do at that time of night and to give me an update in the morning. At breakfast next day, David came to my table and said, "It's OK. Billy came back at 2am. He'd wanted to count the rivets on a bridge structure that we had gone under on the bus and walked back to study it. The only trouble was that he insisted on telling me all about it."

The River Neva runs through St Petersburg and there are a few little beach areas alongside it. They extend only fifty or sixty yards or so and are as little as fifteen yards deep. But the surfaces are just like a beach and the locals love them. The weather was sunny while we were there and a couple of times while we were being driven round the city and passed over the river we saw crowds of local people sitting or standing on one of these beaches sunning themselves. They were totally uninhibited and some of them were naked just trying to benefit from every bit of sun they could.

We drove out of St Petersburg to visit state farms and cooperatives. All were huge and had staff composed of politically appointed managers and lots of labourers. And even though they extended to thousands of acres, they were well over-staffed by Western standards. The other thing that was typical on all the farms I have visited in Soviet-controlled countries was a machinery yard full of old tackle. Also typical was the fact that these old machines were there so that spares could be taken from them to keep the ones being used on the farms going. For it was clear there had been no replacement of tractors, combines or cultivating machinery for years. But it did suggest that the mechanics who managed to keep old machines running were pretty handy and resourceful.

During our tours of northern Russia, we noticed a lack of mature trees in the landscape. Enquiries revealed that virtually every tree had been cut down during the Second World War, either by Russians themselves or by the Germans blockading them. The reasons being in both cases that there was a need for something that would burn to keep them warm during the bitterly cold winters. And remember, the blockade went on for two and a half years. A limited number of trees had been planted since the war but these were only half grown. And any hedges that had been left as divisions between ownerships of land as it became the property of the State had been grubbed up, fields became bigger and divisions were few and far between.

St Petersburg is one of the most sophisticated cities in Russia but even so the food on offer to the general population was pretty basic. Fat pork seemed to be the basis of most meals and people had to queue for it for hours. Of course there was a black market that could supply better stuff at a price.

I well remember on another trip to Russia being invited to the *Financial Times* Moscow correspondent's house for supper one evening. I was writing a weekly column for the paper at the time. He lived in a fairly basic block of flats on the outskirts of Moscow and in view of the things I had seen in the food markets I wondered what his wife would feed me. In the event, we had a delicious leg of lamb with all the trimmings. "Where on earth did you get such meat?" I asked his wife. "I believe it came from Helsinki," she replied. Rudely I asked what it had cost. Reluctantly she told me it had cost her about £50, which, in 1990, was a great deal of money. I hoped her husband's expense account was generous.

However, back to St Petersburg and the party I was leading. We flew from there to Kishinev, the capital of Moldova, still part of the Soviet Union at the time. We arrived in time for the equivalent of our Armistice Day celebrations when people walk and march around wearing all their medals. We went out to see the spectacle and were surprised to see women wearing badges of all kinds that were clearly not for military service. It turned out that they could buy badges showing they were mothers of however many children they'd had and for other things they had done in their lives. They love wearing medals and badges, particularly on that day.

My friend David Chance asked me if I thought he should wear his medal for the Baltic campaign. I replied that of course he should. He took it out of his pocket and pinned it on his lapel and within five minutes he had Moldovans all around him, shaking his hand and thanking him for what he had done. They recognised his medal and what it stood for. It was quite an emotional moment.

From Kishinev we drove the short distance to Chernivtsi in western Ukraine. We were met by the local political head man who was in charge of almost everything in the area. He insisted I ride with him in his 4wd vehicle while the rest of the party followed in the bus.

We went to the local state farm, which the commissar was also in charge of. It was, like the rest of the farms we had seen, huge and over-staffed. We were the first 'white' people they had seen, being so far from Moscow, and they were a bit overwhelmed and possibly frightened by us. You have to remember they had been educated to believe that everybody from the West was their enemy and perestroika had hardly reached Chernivtsi.

They gave us lunch in the canteen. It wasn't very good but we thanked them for it and that broke the ice. Our interpreter worked hard as we engaged the ladies who had served us and their husbands who were the management team, hovered around the tables. Then out to look round the farm.

Once again the commissar insisted I ride with him and the bus followed. As we travelled up a slight hill, we came upon about fifty men leaning on hoes talking and smoking. They should have been hoeing sugar beet but the boss said nothing. When you're working for the government, I suppose you can get away with leaning on hoes. The rest of the farm looked reasonable although the boss told me they could do with rain. Apparently in that part of Ukraine drought is a perennial problem whereas down in the southwest, next to Russia, they have plenty of rain and much better land. It was a surprise to learn that Ukraine is three times as big as France.

Over the course of three days, we got to know the managers on that farm. We found them charming and they realised we didn't have two horns and a tail. On the third day we were presented with a decorated loaf and some salt, which is the traditional way to greet friends in Ukraine. I still have the scarf that the bread was wrapped in. That evening the commissar decided to hold a party for us at our hotel and he invited all the farms' managers and their wives. He hired a band and ordered lots of Stolichnaya vodka. Gorbachev's memo about reducing alcohol consumption had obviously not arrived in Chernivtsi. We were served a very pleasant dinner and after the first course the commissar stood up and toasted our party. Our interpreter whispered to me that I was expected to reply. So, I stood up and toasted the commissar. At which point he stood up and kissed me on both cheeks. I had never been kissed by a man before and didn't like it much. But it set the pattern for the whole evening.

After every course – and there were several – a toast; a reply; and more kissing! Vodka was never my drink of choice but I managed to keep up. The band played and I had to dance with the commissar's little fat wife, and he with mine. I'm not sure what the dances were but I kept to the rhythm and hoped for the best and the little fat wife seemed to enjoy it. Then as I hoped the party was over the commissar proposed one final toast. Once again I had to reply. I had consumed too much vodka but I managed to think of a suitable speech to end the evening.

"Many years ago," I slurred, "we British had a prime minister named Winston Churchill. He coined a phrase to describe the relationship between our two countries. He said there was an iron curtain between us. But, comrades," I said, "this evening that iron curtain has been lifted." *Applause*. "Churchill also spoke of a Cold War that existed between us. But tonight there is no coldness but warmth and friendship." *Toast; more kisses; more applause.* Then my wife led me to bed. But about six months later, Margaret Thatcher, who was the British prime minister who "could do business with Gorbachev", went to Moscow and made the same speech. Except when I made it I was drunk.

A few months later, on the back of the contacts and friends I had made, I took an Anglia TV film crew back to that farm and we filmed the men harvesting sugar beet. The roots were small and the clamps, or heaps of beet, were full of weeds. The hoeing the men had supposedly been doing when I was last there had clearly not been done very well or the weeds would not have been there. But the women of the village, all dressed in ubiquitous headscarves and pinafores, were turning the heaps over pulling all the weeds out so that they didn't block the machines at the processing factory. The whole process was clearly uneconomic but nobody seemed to care. So long as the sugar was sent to Moscow and the people were employed and paid – that was all that mattered. Western management and equipment have gone into those places since then and produced much better crops with far fewer people. A triumph of capitalism over communism I suppose you could call it.

Receiving the decorated loaf and salt. We were honoured

The decorated loaf

The author in Red Square

David Chance, wearing his Baltic medal, Kishinev, Moldova

Contemplating the limited offers on sale, Moscow

The author, posing with commissars, Kishinev , Moldova

Our hotel, Moscow

"Armistice" parade, Kishinev, capital of Moldova

The Summer Palace, St Petersburg

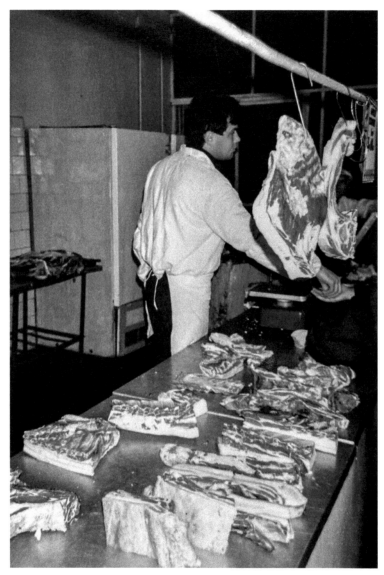

Fat pork! The only meat available

JAPAN

In the early 1990s the British government was blowing rather cold on British agriculture. We'd had a good time since we joined the Common Market (as it was then called) and had, perhaps, overdone production as new techniques were developed. In any event, grain mountains and milk lakes had built up and public perception was that farmers were getting paid subsidised prices for food that nobody wanted. That was an exaggerated view of the situation but perceptions are often more powerful than facts and set-aside – a system of taking land out of production borrowed from America – was introduced. And farming's image had deteriorated.

But in Japan, farmers were being subsidised far more generously than in Europe and yet still enjoyed public support. Why was this? How was Japanese agriculture different from European agriculture? Was it time to try to find out? The answer was yes, and I called Jill Lewis to ask her to arrange a trip there. As usual she obliged and in spring 1994 an AgriTravel party set off for Tokyo.

We were advised that Japanese businessmen like to receive business cards when you meet them and Japan Airlines offered to print a Japanese version of our British cards on the back of our existing versions. I duly sent off a hundred of mine and they came back printed in Japanese. At least that's what I believed, because, surprisingly, I don't speak or read Japanese. And there was no doubt it was good advice. When you meet a Japanese person for the first time they will present you with their card and it is polite to study it – even if you don't understand a word. And they will study your card, not put it in their top pocket without glancing at it. I found, in fact, that most of the people we met had already had their cards printed in English, so full marks Japan Air.

One of the first things you notice about Tokyo is the amount of neon lights. They flash everywhere in different colours and different languages. That is to say, some of the flashes were in Japanese but many more were in English, or possibly American. Walking the streets soon after we arrived it was clear that the Japanese enjoy gambling. There were dozens of premises full of one-armed bandits and every seat seemed occupied. Another preoccupation was karaoke. You could see and hear Japanese people singing along to Frank Sinatra, Cliff Richard, Elvis Presley and so on. The hotels were great. One we stayed in had a huge reception with a big picture window outside of which was a waterfall reaching the full height of the window. And across the reception area was a winding stream of running water. The rooms were nice too. The bathroom was divided from the bedroom by a see-through panel, which was alright until you wanted some privacy, and the toilet had buttons alongside the seat so that you could choose which service you required. I will say no more.

While we were in Tokyo, I had arranged to interview the Japanese minister of agriculture. I was writing a regular column for the *Financial Times* and I thought his views might be of interest to our readers. I had organised the Tokyo correspondent of the paper to be my interpreter and she turned up at the ministry as arranged. As an aside, by coincidence just across the road from the agriculture building, Shoko Asahara, leader of the Aum cult, who had earlier masterminded the poisoning of some underground stations with sarin gas, was being taken in handcuffs to the main Tokyo police station.

The lady who was to act as my interpreter and I waited in the reception until we were called. She was Japanese although dressed like an American and she spoke English with an American accent. She was obviously bright. You don't get to work for the *Financial Times* if you're not and we had a useful conversation as I told her the kind of questions I would ask the minister. She treated me as an equal, as I did her, and I enjoyed speaking to her. Then we were called upstairs to the minister's office. Suddenly she became a totally different person. She bowed low in front of the minister and lowered her voice to a whisper. She treated him like a god and I soon became sure that the questions I asked her to put to him had been edited down in her mind before she asked them. Politicians of any race are adept at avoiding answers to questions and this man was no exception. But most of the responses I got were useless because the Japanese class system stopped her asking direct questions.

I got a few quotes from the minister but it was not a successful session and I was disappointed. We returned to the ground floor and out of the building and she reverted to her bright personality. It was like turning a tap on and off and it gave me an insight to the Japanese way of life. I witnessed the same kind of class distinction at businesses we visited later on the tour although not as pronounced. The class system is alive and well in Japan.

Our bus eventually escaped the Tokyo traffic and we started to explore the main island of Honshu. But we hadn't gone far before our route was blocked. Apparently a bridge had been demolished by a recent earthquake and it had not yet been rebuilt. Regular earthquakes were another aspect of Japan that I had not fully appreciated. One of the first farms we visited reared Wagyu beef. The first Wagyu animals had already appeared in Britain although most of us had not seen them. They are a traditional Japanese breed famous for their marbled meat. The tradition also claims that this marbling is enhanced by daily massages with beer. But we saw no animals being massaged. And the animals themselves were quite good looking but not outstanding in their conformation. Later in the tour we had a chance to taste the meat and it was good – but very expensive.

We were already becoming aware of how small the farms are. Rice paddies that have to be flooded can't be very big, of course, or it wouldn't be possible to flood them evenly. But many paddies are no more than garden size. And most of the work was being done by hand by both men and women. Some of our questions were beginning to be answered. If such small holdings were not heavily subsidised, they would not survive economically. And visits to some of these small farms confirmed the traditional nature of what they did and why their way of life was revered by the population as a whole.

We paused at one point for another tradition – the Japanese tea ceremony. The rules were quite strict. We had to file into the room where it was to take place quietly with no chatter and kneel on the floor around it in an orderly fashion. Almost like going into church. Then the geisha appeared, complete with a long traditional costume with a wide belt around her waist and some sort of roll of material stuffed in the back of it. She almost appeared to worship the tea as she prepared it on her knees and then carefully served small cups with no handles to each person. We had to pick up our cup with both hands and sip. It was a bit like the green tea I had had in China and I was no more impressed with this than when I was there. But I'm probably being churlish. The tradition is the thing, not the taste, and we had just witnessed and been a part of an ancient rite, so should be glad.

As we travelled around, we were on the lookout for traditional Japanese architecture. Amazingly there is quite a bit of it – great curved overhanging eaves surmounting different levels of the main structures. Predictably, some of these beautiful buildings have been replaced by steel and concrete but even many of them have had traditional-looking roofs superimposed on them. We admired them very much.

We had been told that the main island for agriculture as we would understand it was Hokkaido so it was our next stop. Sure enough we found cereals and sugar beet as well as slightly bigger paddy fields. We also found a support system for local farmers of which our farming colleagues at home would be envious. We visited a centre to which farmers could apply for advice. It was staffed by extension officers with detailed knowledge of the area and these were supported by field officers who kept them in touch with plant diseases as they occurred. This was one of a network of similar centres across Hokkaido to advise and help farmers with their decision making.

Farmers are obsessed with the weather, of course, and one service available to local farmers around that advisory station was live weather forecasting based on satellite photography and transmitted to a TV screen. This kind of service enabling a farmer to know within a few minutes when rain or sunshine is going to reach his land is commonplace nowadays and we see it daily on our TV forecasting. But this was 1994 and those farmers had access to this technology 24/7 years before it reached the UK.

On our last night in Japan we were taken to a traditional Japanese restaurant. I don't think any of us realised what we were in for until we got to the room where it was to be served and had to take our shoes off and leave them outside the door. Inside we found a table about a foot (25cm) high. In other words, we had to sit on our haunches and pick our food off the low table, with chopsticks. It was one of the most uncomfortable meals I have ever eaten. The food was fine – a mixture of tempura and sushi which most of us could manage. We had a lot of laughs and some of us found a wall to lean against which helped a lot.

Towards the end of the evening one member of our party, a strawberry grower from near Birmingham, got up and left the room. A call of nature I assumed. He was gone a long while but that's understandable in a foreign country. At last he came back but could hardly contain himself with laughter. It turned out that there were several other parties in other rooms each with their shoes outside their doors. He had decided to mix them all up and said we should probably retrieve ours to prevent others knowing who the culprit was. I'm not sure what his antics did for Anglo/Japanese relations but watching the other diners scrambling around the place for their shoes gave us Brits the biggest laugh of the trip.

Precision farming

Wagyu cattle

Wonderful ornate roofs everywhere

Japanese gardens are so beautiful

Geisha girl

Next page: Rice paddy Hokkaido

Training tomatoes

Tea ceremony

The party that went to Japan

SOUTH AMERICA

On April 2nd, 1982, Argentina invaded the Falkland Islands, or as the Argentinians called them, the Malvinas. They were, and are, British, even though they are far away in the South Atlantic. But Argentina had long insisted they belonged to their country and President Galtieri, the dictator newly ruling Argentina, needed a means to unite his cash-strapped nation. He decided on the classic ploy to try to create loyalty behind what he believed would be a popular policy and sent his troops to invade Port Stanley, the capital of the Falklands. Britain had only a few soldiers there and certainly not enough to repel a full-scale invasion and so the British Governor of the Islands, Rex Hunt, had no alternative but to surrender.

Ten weeks later, on June 14th, after much hasty preparation, long sea journeys and many soldiers' deaths and woundings on both sides, the Falklands War was over and the British were once again installed as rulers. Margaret Thatcher, the prime minister, was triumphant and won a General Election on the back of the victory. But there was no doubt the British government had been caught unprepared. Galtieri was tried in Buenos Aires and imprisoned. And before long everything seemed to settle down to the way the two country's relationships had been before.

A few years later, in the mid 1980s, it seemed to me a good time to take a look at Argentina. A few people wondered if we'd be welcome but it didn't take long for Jill Lewis to get a party together and we set off on a plane via Madrid to Buenos Aires. It was a long journey which made us feel for the soldiers, sailors and airmen who had sailed and flown to recapture the Falklands a few years earlier. When we boarded the plane in Madrid for the longest leg of the journey, one member of our party asked if I minded if he tried to get himself upgraded. He'd had a recent knee operation. He was Anthony Gurney, a Norfolk farmer, an ex-military man and a descendent of the Gurneys who helped found Barclays Bank in Norwich. I told him to go ahead and wished him luck.

This was just before the days when pilots were locked away at the front of a plane to foil potential hijackers. Ten minutes later, Anthony came back to me in the steerage part of the plane and said, "It's OK David, I've got a seat in first class. I know the pilot's father." And he disappeared with his hand luggage to the front of the plane.

On the bus from Buenos Aires airport tour to our hotel, Anthony came to see me again. "Are you going straight to bed?" he asked. I replied that after a twenty-hour journey I was tired and yes that was my intention. "Well, if you have the energy I have arranged to meet some friends at the hotel and I'd like you to meet them." Somewhat reluctantly, I made my way to the hotel bar and there was Anthony with the captain of the Argentinian polo team and his two strapping sons who had driven three hours across the Pampas to meet him. They were charming people and despite my tiredness I enjoyed a few drinks with them. Apparently, Anthony had played polo with the eldest of the three in India. Of course he had. It isn't what you know, it's who you know.

Anthony became a great friend and was one of the members of the cooperative buying group, Loddon Farmers, of which I was chairman. He may well pop up again in this narrative.

In Buenos Aires we visited the grave of Eva Perón, one of the favourite spots for tourists to aim for thanks to Tim Rice and Andrew Lloyd Webber, and also the square and the balcony from which she proclaimed her love for her country. Then back to farming. On the outskirts of Buenos Aires is a huge cattle market called Liniers. On the day we visited there were *only* 28,000 cattle to sell. The market's capacity was 40,000. The cattle, raised and fattened on the pampas grass that dominated the landscape in a semicircle with a radius of more than 300 miles around Buenos Aires (which is on the coast), were brought to the market and offered for sale to meat buyers. Penned in lots of up to fifty animals, they were herded at speed along gangways between the pens by cowboys on fantastic quarter horses that seemed to be able to read the minds of the cattle. And they were sold in covered rings by a team of auctioneers whose patter would not have been understood by us Brits even if we spoke Spanish.

It was quite an experience for our party. We'd never seen anything like it and we were able to walk along the buyers' walkways above the animals and judge their finish. Most of the cattle were Hereford or Aberdeen Angus or crosses between them so we could bask in the fact that, at one time, long ago, Britain had been the stock farm of the world and supplied breeding animals to places like Argentina. In the cafés around the market, buyers mixed with drovers and shared little pots of maté, a kind of thick tea in a little pot sucked through a metal straw. It was, I'm afraid, an acquired taste and I declined the offer of a suck a few times. But the locals didn't seem to be able to do without it.

About ten years later, I enthusiastically went back to Liniers with another party promising them a wonderful experience. But it didn't seem like the same place. Only 6,000 cattle were there – and when you consider the capacity of 40,000 the pens looked almost empty. And this was now normal, not just an unfortunate day, as I found when I asked what had happened. The Argentinian government, facing another perennial crisis, had imposed a punitive tax on beef exports in order to raise money for its administration. This had resulted in a loss on every animal and most of the farmers on the Pampas had stopped producing beef cattle and ploughed up their grass. What I was seeing on that second visit was a dying industry – one that had sustained Argentina for many decades. Furthermore, I learned that Argentina was now not self-sufficient for beef and was importing supplies from neighbouring Uruguay.

We went out into what had been the Pampas the next day and where there had been thousands of acres of rich grazing there were thousands of acres of land growing soya beans. I enquired how many soya beans Argentina consumed and was told almost none. So what happens to them? Oh, they're exported to China. Next question: every field appears to be growing soya beans. You can only grow them once every five years if you want to avoid devastating diseases like sclerotinia. So where are the other crops such as cereals to spread the rotation? Answer: we're continuously cropping with soya. It's the only crop that is profitable.

My reply to such an answer was that the farmers were playing with fire. That they may be able to get away with continuous cropping for a few years because of the latent fertility left in the soil by the grass that had been left undisturbed for generations. But sooner or later the plant diseases would get them. I have not been back recently to check whether my forecast was accurate but I fear it might have been and that they won't be able to produce viable soya if it was. It is an illustration of how governments impose policies that have unintended consequences.

But to return to my first visit. We were entertained royally by the Argentinian farmers. There was no shortage of beef then. We would turn up, after eating steaks for breakfast in our hotel, be driven round the farms on trailers, inspecting the crops and the cattle as we came to them. The stock, usually Hereford types, would be driven to us by a few cowboys on more beautiful quarter horses. Then back to the hacienda – all were beautifully designed houses that suited their environment perfectly with balconies and rooms with high ceilings, for a drink before lunch. A fire would be lit in the garden, a mesh of steel placed over it and very soon the smell of barbecued beef would come wafting towards us. The hosts would then serve us huge steaks. We had never eaten so much beef in our lives. And we knew we would probably be served the same again for dinner in our hotel. Belts were fully extended by the end of that trip.

One of the things I had warned our party was that our hosts might be sensitive about the Falklands. Best not to mention the war, I'd said. How wrong I was. Most of the people we visited told us they were pleased we (the British) had "got rid of Galtieri for us". They still felt the Malvina's belonged to Argentina but they held no grudges even though it was only a few years since the war. And our hosts were universally generous and pleased to welcome us.

We were scheduled to fly across the country to the edge of the Andes but before we did we went to see the Iguazu Falls. They – and there are many across the complex – are probably the biggest waterfalls in the world; taller than Niagara and wider than Victoria, and awe-inspiring in every sense. They are half in Argentina and half in the Brazilian state of Parana and we approached the hotel where we would stay the night on the Brazilian side. One of the notable things about this southern part of Brazil was the number of unfinished houses along the roads. Our guide told us this was probably because the builders had run out of money and left them unfinished until they were able to afford the materials. "They'll be back once they have the money," he said.

Our first view of the falls was from a hill above them where we could see the great expanse of the Iguazu River that broadened like a sea before tumbling over the rocks into the pools below. We could also see a long row of hydroelectric turbines that supplied electricity to large areas of Argentina as well as the south of Brazil. Alongside the turbines stood several trucks that were dwarfed by the turbines and, from where we stood, looked like Dinky Toys. In other words, the entire vista was huge and it's no surprise that it has been named a World Heritage Site.

The hotel was much closer to the action and there was a wooden walkway leading across the face of the falls. The noise of the water was deafening as you walked along it and yet there were little birds flying under the flow where it looked as if they had nests in the cliff. And on bushes nearby were blue butterflies, hundreds of them, with a wingspan as big as your hand. The whole experience was overwhelming and has stuck in my mind ever since.

Next, a flight west to Mendoza at the eastern edge of the Andes. The region is famous for wine and grows a large percentage of the country's production. Sheltered by the mountains, grapes thrive on Mendoza's slopes enabling Argentina to be the fifth largest wine producer in the world. We were treated to an obligatory wine tasting and were agreeably surprised at the quality of what we were offered.

And after an enjoyable stay in the region, we set off by bus over the Andes to Santiago, capital of Chile.

Iguazu falls

Iguazu falls

The walkways are an ideal way to view the cattle

The pens went on into the middle distance

Liniers Market, Buenos Aires. Our party were fascinated by the cattle and the horse riding drovers

There were huge pale blue butterflies

Before we set off, our driver said he hoped none of us had a heart condition because we would be going quite high and that could have a nasty effect on the vulnerable. "But I've got some oxygen on board so don't worry." It was an exciting ride. The higher we went, the more we could see the minerals in the rocks. Bright reds and golds and everything in between. One day, I thought, someone will come and mine these hills. We also saw a few condors, huge birds with broad wingspans flying above us which gave us a thrill. Then one of our party members passed out. He'd had heart problems back home, his wife told us, and the emergency oxygen had to be brought up from the hold. Fortunately it revived him and we were soon to start descending into Chile, so panic over, although a few of us developed temporary headaches which is one of the symptoms of altitude sickness.

One of the things I had not expected was the German influence in Chile. A fair bit of German money had been invested in Chilean industry and we even came across a few expat German farmers. The whole country looked more prosperous and in better shape than its eastern neighbour. And Santiago was a fine city. Jumping forward a few years, I was there with another party a few years later just after an earthquake and it was sad to see parts of the city's buildings scattered over the pavements where they fell.

On that occasion, we had approached Chile from further south on the edge of Patagonia. Coming from Argentina, we had arrived at a city called Bariloche, a thousand miles west of Buenos Aires and halfway up an Ande if you get my drift. It's a truly beautiful area and has been named a national park by the Argentinian government. We stayed there one night before our crossing into Chile. About 3.30am the windows of the hotel bedroom shook like crazy. It woke up both myself and my wife and she said, "What on earth was that?" "I expect it was the wind," I replied, "go back to sleep."

But it wasn't wind. It was an earthquake in the Pacific that had caused a tsunami on Chilean beaches and quite a lot of damage on the mainland. Our rattling windows were the result of being on the edge of the affected area. Some members of the party I was leading had been glued to their televisions half the night and at breakfast told me we should book a plane and go home – not even attempt to cross into Chile. I told them to wait until I could assess the situation over there and made some calls on my mobile phone.

We had arranged for a guide in Chile and I called her to enquire about the situation. "Don't worry," she said. "We're used to earthquakes. Our farmers are looking forward to seeing you. I will meet you at the ferry as arranged." I went back to the party and told them what I'd heard. Some of them took a while to calm down but eventually I persuaded everybody to stay with the programme. And it was a very attractive programme. For, crossing the Andes at that point involved catching ferry boats across four high-altitude lakes with bus transport between them. It was really quite romantic, except the porters, who moved cases on and off ferries all day and every day, did not care how much damage they did to ours and some of them took a pounding.

However, we met our guide as planned and she reassured the nervous among us that all would be fine. There was only one problem and that was at a vineyard we had been scheduled to visit. They could not now take us because the quake had smashed most of their bottles. A bus took us north along the main motorway and at one point was slowed down by a policeman. The earthquake had caused a crack right across the road over a bridge and a sheet of thick flat steel had been placed over it so we could cross it with care. We did so with no bother and I thought to myself if that had happened at home the road would have been closed for a year.

We later went to one dairy farm where, as a result of a previous earthquake, they had lost electrical power for three days and had been unable to milk their cows. This had caused stress to the cows and loss of income to the farmer. Cows subjected to that kind of treatment never return to the amount of milk they were yielding before, never mind the big loss on the days no milk could be sold. But as our guide had told us, Chileans are used to earthquakes and have learned to improvise.

We were scheduled to fly home from Santiago and there were rumours that the airport there had suffered severe damage. Once again, the nervous members of our party started to panic. But when we reached the airport ready to book in for our flight to London, sure enough the terminal was so badly damaged with fallen masonry all around the place that it was unusable. No problem. The airport staff had erected a marquee in the car park and we checked-in in that. Once again, I was full of admiration for Chile.

However, we were there to look at farms as well as quake damage and one impressive dairy farm we went to had a large herd of fine-looking cows and also grew broccoli for European supermarkets. The main story I remember from that farm was that they were required by the supermarkets to cut the broccoli into lengths that would fit into the boxes stipulated. We all know that story. But making the product fit the boxes meant a lot of waste. So they decided to feed the waste to their cows. It appeared to be working well. The cows liked the broccoli – which is more than I do – but more and more of them refused to breed. It took their vet a long while to decide this must be because of the broccoli. They stopped feeding it and the cows began breeding normally again. The law of unintended consequences.

One evening, the hotel in which we were staying had a poster behind the reception desk advertising a horse show in a local arena. "That looks interesting," someone said, "maybe we should go to it." At which the receptionist piped up, "Don't bother, all the seats will be sold by now." Anthony Gurney (remember him?) joined the conversation at that point and said we should give it a try. So we booked a few taxis to take those who wanted to join to the arena. We arrived there a few minutes later to find hordes of people going through the turnstiles. Anthony called out, "Follow me!" and set off to one of the entry points. When he got to the gate he said to the person in charge, "We're the English party. OK," and beckoned us all through behind him. The turnstile operator stood there open-mouthed and let us all through without paying a cent. We found our way up to the bench seats and were very soon having conversations with local people. Indeed, they insisted on sharing their sandwiches with us. The horses and their riders performed their tricks and it was a very enjoyable evening. Once again Anthony had come up trumps.

Looking up some of the details of Chile while we were there, I discovered that the country is about 2,650 miles long, north to south and averages 110 miles wide, east to west, which is, to say the least, an odd shape for a country. And it sits on something called the Nazca Plate which moves 10cm east per year. Hence the regular earthquakes and also hence how the Andes have been pushed up from the sea over millions of years. Indeed, the long east coast of Chile, along the southern Pacific, is like a great big beach. And it was this same characteristic of land that was one of the reasons why, on another occasion, I chose to visit Peru and Ecuador because they share the same kind of geology.

I had a friend who grew a large acreage of asparagus in Britain and over dinner one evening he had told me he had invested in an asparagus farm in Peru. He explained that it was possible to produce fresh asparagus all the year round there and that labour was so much cheaper there that it more than offset the costs of flying it to the UK. He also spoke of other fruit and vegetables that were being grown in Peru and that in his view it was set to become one of Europe's biggest suppliers of out-of-season produce. This called for another phone call to my friend Jill Lewis at AgriTravel and in February 2002 another touring party set off for Lima.

One of the first places we visited was the International Potato Center. It's sometimes forgotten that the potato originated from the Andes and the tubers we consume every day are descended from those grown wild in this unlikely area. But the Center reminds us of this history and continues to experiment with new varieties and strains. Some of the strange-coloured potatoes we saw there appeared to have scant relationship to Maris Piper or King Edward or one of the other popular varieties we eat every day. But Peruvian scientists are constantly working to establish varieties that are resistant to diseases which can then be crossed with potatoes grown around the world and, over time, transfer such resistance to them.

Then down to the 'beach' to my friend's asparagus farm. The soil, if you could call it that, was pure sand. And it stretched for miles inland, having, as previously noted, been pushed up from the sea. This combination of sand, sunshine (Peru is very close to the equator) and irrigation (there is plenty of water running down in rivers from snow melt in the Andes), enables crops of asparagus to be grown multiple times per year, unprotected by glass or plastic. So, instead of, say, two and a half to three tonnes per acre, typical in Britain, the Peruvians could grow ten tonnes per acre. And trials were being conducted that indicated much more than that was possible. In addition, as my friend had told me, the cost of labour was a fraction of what he had to pay in Britain. It was all very impressive but what did Peruvian asparagus taste like? We were given some to try and while it still had the traditional taste it seemed to me less intense than what I would expect from homegrown. But as we have seen since 2002 that has not put off UK consumers who now buy Peruvian asparagus all year long.

We went to a farm growing roses on an industrial scale. All were for export and most would end up in the Clock Auction in Holland having been flown in to Schiphol and been pushed through the tunnel to the auction. It has established itself as the main redistribution point for flowers in the world. Back on the farm in Peru, the roses were grown on a field scale and cut by hand for specific markets. For instance, the Russian market demands mainly red roses with long stems and sold as single blooms. So, there was one packing line preparing roses to suit that market. The British, on the other hand, like a mixture of colours, with much shorter stems and sold in bunches of ten or twelve. Another packing line was working on that and so on. I'd had no idea different countries had different likes in colours and presentation of flowers. You learn something new every day.

We certainly did when we visited a farm that bred alpacas, which are native to the Andes as are their larger cousins, llamas. The farm was run by a vet and her daughter and they were keen on selling us overpriced garments made of alpaca fibre. We were escorted into their house that had been converted into an alpaca garment showroom and we were lectured on how warm the garments were and how fashionable. In passing, the lady claimed what wonderful companion animals alpacas were, which I found slightly ridiculous and said so. But she insisted and said they were being used by specialists to help sick and disturbed people to recover.

A little later we were invited to go out onto a nearby meadow where about twenty-five alpacas were grazing. The animals were not shy of humans and sniffed around us before going back to graze. But one of them identified that a member of our party was blind and had a damaged face. Without any urging by anyone, this alpaca attached itself to Tony and licked his hands and then his face. It stood there almost cuddling Tony, if that were possible, for at least fifteen minutes and Tony stroked it and cried. Some of us did too. It was an emotional moment and I had to revise my opinion about companion animals, at least with regard to that particular alpaca.

We visited other farms growing avocados, grapes, tangerines and passion fruit and at one point ran into an inspector from Marks & Spencer, there to ensure the stores' standards were upheld, with particular attention, it seemed to us, that the farm was not employing child labour. Doubtless he checked the picking and packing lines for cleanliness but they seemed less important to him than children. Child labour had been in the UK news just before we were there and his visit seemed less a food safety check and more a PR exercise.

You cannot visit Peru without going to Machu Picchu and we were no exception. So, back on the bus and off up the hill – 11,000 feet up the hill to be precise. At first sight you think what a stupid place to build a city. Then you are reminded that the Incas were sun worshippers and their religion demanded they get as close to the object of their worship as possible. It was, in its day, and judging by the extent of its ruins, a sizeable settlement. And to feed the people who lived there they created terraces of soil on which to grow crops. It can't have been an easy life and must have involved a great deal of climbing up and down rocks. But religious fervour makes people do strange things even today and it must have been the same a few thousand years ago.

On the same day as we went to Machu Picchu, we went to Cusco, a city situated at a similar high altitude and also built many years ago by a branch of the Incas. Its stone-based architecture was precise and featured, among other things, windows in perfect symmetry with one another so that you could look through one and see clearly through several others. The houses had elegant courtyards with arches separating open areas from broad passages and the roads between buildings were rocks laid with precision. Altogether it was an inspiring place and the dwellings of the natives – I'm not sure if I should call them South American Indians – were crude by comparison.

We went to a high-altitude village to see for ourselves how they lived. Men seemed thin on the ground, or perhaps they were hiding as their women folk entertained us. They dressed in what looked like layers of blouses topped off with shawls tied around their necks. On their heads they wore what looked like baskets turned upside down, tied with ribbon under their chins. Their skin, even the relatively young ones, was leathery and lined, an inevitable complexion, I suppose, when you lived more than 11,000 feet above sea level in temperatures that must vary from very hot to very cold on the same day. Some of them invited us into their houses that were as basic on the inside as they were on the outside. In the kitchen of the house that I went in, I suddenly felt something running over my feet. I thought it must be a cat but when I checked it was a guinea pig, one of several running around on the floor. On enquiring I was told guinea pigs are kept to eat, and live with the family eating scraps off the floor. When they want meat for Sunday lunch the woman of the house picks a guinea pig, kills and skins it and roasts it in the oven. The shortest food chain you could ever imagine.

One matter I have not mentioned until now is the problems we had in the trouser department. In other words, several of us were creating a fair bit of slurry. The food had seemed clean and hygienically served but it had upset some of our stomachs and we dared not stray far from a lavatory. Fortunately, the bus was equipped with one but to say it was cramped and uncomfortable would be an understatement. Furthermore, the bus driver was not keen for us to use the facility because he had to clean it out every evening. However, Montezuma's revenge was relentless and needs must, despite many Imodium pills being swallowed.

We took our tummy problems north into Ecuador and some of us felt well below par when we reached Quito. But our Ecuadorian guide, named Marisol, soon cheered us up and we continued with our adventure. We stayed mainly in haciendas which the owners had converted for touristic use. Like us, they needed to diversify away from farming to make a decent living and they were simply using the assets they had to hand. It was a real privilege to sit and eat dinner with such people and hear their family stories.

Ecuador is, of course, on the equator and we took advantage of that to stand on the actual line, or that's what it was claimed to be. Very touristy. And one of our hacienda hosts laid on a bit more touristy entertainment. He got all his gauchos and their horses to give us a demonstration of their skills. Roping calves, lassoing grown cattle, rounding up bunches of cows and so on. It made for an enjoyable evening and one enterprising lady who was part of our group had a go at some of the tricks. She did pretty well too.

In the equatorial climate you can grow practically anything so long as you have water and there is plenty of that. We saw more flowers for export, also scheduled to fly to the Dutch market, bananas and coffee, that I'd expected to find in Brazil (and I did, on another trip, so please be patient). And we saw dairy farms and beef farms with all the animals being fed on irrigated grass. It had been a long tour (three weeks) and I had business to attend to at home, so Lorna and I flew back early while most of the rest of the party extended their tour by ship to the Galapagos Islands where Darwin developed his book on the origin of the species. I was really sorry to miss that experience but business called and I had to enjoy it, vicariously, through their accounts when they got back.

A few years later, the TV news was full of accounts of how the Brazilian rainforest was being burned to provide more space to raise cattle and what this meant to the rest of the world. It was the year 2000 and the real beginning of the serious climate change debate that has continued ever since and it seemed to me time to go and see if it was all true. Jill Lewis said she had a contact in Rio de Janeiro and set about organising a tour for us. By this time we had a reasonably loyal following of people like ourselves who appreciated an active, informative tour rather than sitting on a beach for two weeks, so we soon put a party together.

First stop was Rio itself. We were booked into a hotel on Copacabana beach and despite what I said about beaches, Lorna and I could not resist taking our shoes off and walking down to the water. We hadn't reckoned on how hot the sand was but our feet soon acclimatised and on we threaded our way through the young people frolicking there wearing the smallest bikinis I had ever seen. Postage stamps would have been a better description. I didn't know where to look. Clearly this was no place for a middle-aged, overweight farmer but I believe one or two of our party braved ridicule and took a dip.

We retired to the hotel to recover from jetlag and opted for an early night thinking what an attractive place it was. Next morning at breakfast we learned that during the night a man had been shot and killed about a hundred yards from the hotel, which kinda made you think twice about going out after dark. However, we were all fine and ready for our introduction to Brazil. Our guide was the very attractive, middle-aged lady who knew Jill but she was extremely bossy. In fact, one of our party christened her 'Gruppen Fuhrer'. Not so she could hear it, of course. She would not have appreciated that.

But she shared some vital information with us. The language spoken in Brazil is Portuguese, which seems odd with Argentina speaking Spanish next door. The difference relates to which European country first invaded the territory. It was the Spanish who invaded Argentina and the Portuguese who invaded Brazil in the early part of the 16th century. And while it still seems strange when you see it on a map it makes more sense when you account for the size of South America, which is huge. And Brazil takes up almost half of it. The population of the country is roughly made up of 35% white descendants of the Portuguese conquerors and 65% black or mixed race who are the descendants of Africans brought there by Portuguese ships as slaves.

We did, of course, do a few touristy things, like climbing the Corcovado mountain to see the massive statue of Christ the Redeemer and we took the cable car up Sugar Loaf Mountain from where you get a panoramic view of all Rio's magnificent beaches. There were crowds, but it was worth it for the views. Then back to serious farming. We flew from Rio to Cuiabá in the state of Mato Grosso. It's the third biggest state in Brazil but contains only about 1.6% of the population. It was one of the areas which used to be covered by rainforest and savannah but much of which has now been taken over by agriculture.

We visited one of the biggest farms in the state. It was situated on a large flat plateau and was, until a few years previously, all savannah – in other words natural grassland in which trees are widely spaced and which supports wild grazing animals and indigenous tribes. We had heard stories about the owner of this farm before we got there. Apparently, he had been the pioneer developer and had driven the indigenous population away from the area, sometimes with guns. He had persuaded some of his friends to join him and they had cleared the land and between them amassed thousands of acres of farming land. It needed lime to counteract acidity which had to be brought in from other regions in Brazil but apart from that it was good to grow crops of maize, soya bean and coffee. And as we travelled from the airport, we saw those crops as far as the eye could see.

I asked the manager of one farm about conservation which we had been assured was being protected by government decree. "Oh yes," he said with a grin. "Twenty per cent of our land stays wild." "So," I asked, "where is it?" "Oh, it's over the hill in that direction," pointing vaguely. I said there were no hills and he responded by saying, "I thought you were here to look at crops?" In other words, it probably didn't exist. So much for government decrees. But we had to admit the crops looked fantastic. And we could not ignore the fact that these people had come to this area and built a town complete with shops, schools, churches and houses for the workers on land where there had been nothing but mud huts before they came.

The owner of the biggest farm invited us round to his house for tea and cakes in the afternoon. And he and his wife were most hospitable. But the gates to the property were guarded by four armed guards and there were high fences with razor wire all around it. He had achieved his ambition to farm many thousands of acres but he was obviously concerned about his safety and security.

We stayed in the state for a couple of days and visited a pig farm. As a lifelong pig keeper myself, I was intrigued to see sows and their piglets in open-sided pens. The weather was so mild, year-round, that they needed no protection, no heat lamps like we have to provide in the UK and were doing very well. Like everything else in the area, the pig herd was many thousands strong and we began to appreciate how Brazil had become one of the biggest producers and exporters of food products in the world.

We stayed a couple of nights in a basic but adequate hotel and on the first morning as we were to continue our tour of Mato Grosso we were hurried onto the bus by the Gruppen Fuhrer because she thought we would be late for our next appointment. And she told the driver to go, go, go. Lorna asked her if we were all aboard and she replied that of course we were and off we went. Several miles down the road Lorna had a sixth sense that someone was missing and walked to the back of the bus and counted the party. Sure enough, we were one short. The Gruppen Fuhrer checked and had to admit Lorna was right and we had to turn round and retrace our steps. When we got back to the hotel there stood the missing passenger waiting for a taxi he had ordered. His name must stay anonymous but he was a middle-aged divorcee. He had been phoning his new girlfriend in England and the connection from that remote area had taken longer than he anticipated.

We flew south to Sao Paulo, the most populous city in Brazil. It is famous for its carnival, not least because of the high proportion of black people who live there but we had missed that celebration. We did, however, tour the city and its prosperous centre full of high-rise offices and flats as well as the favelas on its outskirts. These are essentially huts on the hills around the city where thousands, perhaps millions, of people live in squalor. It demonstrated as nothing else could the difference between the white Portuguese business owners and their mainly black workers. I wondered if it was very different from the days of slavery. It was no surprise that there was a high crime rate.

All around the city were more traditional farms than we had seen in Mato Grosso. They'd been established far longer and produced a wider variety of crops. One farm we went to produced cereals, citrus fruits, soya beans, sugar cane and coffee. Some of these were new to me and as a sugar beet grower in the UK I was interested to see the cane grown and harvested. Obviously the crops look very different in the field but once harvested it seemed to me the process of extracting the sugar was very similar. In both cases, the crop is chopped and then boiled to wash out the sweet juices and this liquid sugar is then crystalised in centrifuges into granules. I already knew that once processed, the end product of both are virtually indistinguishable from one another.

I was even more interested in coffee. I had a son in the coffee business and had heard a lot about it from him. But there is no substitute to seeing something yourself. So, from the beginning – coffee beans are grown on bushes that are perennial. They can be harvested by machine or by hand. The coffee cherries are spread thinly over large areas of flat ground or concrete and left to dry in the sun. As they dry the soft cherry flesh turns into dry chaff (or cascara) leaving the two halves of the pip - and these two halves are what we know as green coffee beans. They have distinct flavour characteristics according to where they have been grown and coffee beans are the biggest traded commodity for human consumption in the world. The only commodities traded in greater volume are petroleum products but they don't taste as good. And I assume green coffee beans are traded in even bigger quantities these days since Howard Shultz opened a coffee bar called Starbucks in Seattle the 1980's and started a worldwide craze for coffee.

We also went to a coffee processing plant nearby where beans were being sorted and roasted but the main product was instant coffee sold in bottles or tins ready to spoon into hot water. It was all very impressive until I saw a man sweeping the floor and tipping it into the bin from which the containers were filled. I pointed this out to the guide and he replied that it didn't matter because all beans for instant coffee were the lowest quality and anyway the floor was pretty clean.

We visited a cattle farm where there was a large herd of Nelore cows. These are the animals bred specifically for the tropics in India, with a hump above their shoulders. I'm not sure what purpose the hump serves but we were told they have excellent mothering qualities, they have good growth rates and when slaughtered have a good ratio of meat to bone, known as the killing out percentage. They can also tolerate high temperatures given where they came from and so are well suited to a country like Brazil and we were told the number of Nelore herds was growing fast. Another reminder of Brazil's expansion as a world food supplier. Indeed, it is already the world's biggest supplier of chicken meat. And the thing is they grow all the ingredients for feeding the multiple species they produce within their own boundary.

My friend Alan Alston, sadly no longer with us, and our wives went shopping when we visited the city of Porto Alegre towards the south of Brazil. The ladies found a shopping mall that was obviously going to amuse them for some time, so Alan and I found a park bench on which to wait for them. Two young ladies were already sitting at the other end of the bench and after a while one of them said in what sounded like a French accent, "Excuse me, are you gentlemen English?" We replied that, yes, we were. "May I ask which part of England you come from?" the girl continued. We replied that we came from a county she'd probably never heard of called Norfolk. "Oh yes, I have been there," she replied. "Are you anywhere near Thetford?" "Well, yes we were. It's just up the road from where we live." And it turned out that she had been 'best friend' of the son of a farming friend of ours and had visited him the previous year. What a small world we live in.

Before we came home, we took a short side trip to Uruguay. It is one of the smallest countries in South America just north of Buenos Aires and its capital is Montevideo, situated on the delta of the River Plate. We were told that around 90% of the land in Uruguay is pasture and we saw vast herds of cattle grazing the gentle hills. And we remembered it was the home of the, by then, defunct Fray Bentos meat factory that produced cans of corned beef. It may be small but it is a beautiful country. One area we drove through was nicknamed Little Switzerland and that description fitted it perfectly. We went to look at some first-class beef cattle and we were entertained generously by the farmer and his wife. We got the impression they were really glad to see us.

That impression was confirmed even more when we took a long bus ride down the coast to see some Texel sheep breeders. Their community was, to say the least, isolated and we began to wonder when we would arrive at the venue, which was a small market complete with a sale ring. But when we arrived, we were overwhelmed by the welcome the breeders gave us. There were forty or fifty farmers and their wives all dressed up in their Sunday best and they had brought a selection of their stock for us to inspect. When we had done that, assessing the quality of the animals, and posed for press photos by the reporter who was present, we were ushered into the sale ring where the wives had laid out a spread for us complete with lots of English and Uruguayan flags. We suspected their isolation meant that they didn't get many visitors. But they certainly welcomed us – almost embarrassingly so. I vowed to go back to Uruguay one day.

Lorna and me either side of the Equator - note the line in the floor

Coffee beans on the bush

There's an awful lot of coffee in Brazil

A coffee drying floor. The beans are spread out to dry in the sun

The terraces for growing food at Machu Picchu - carved out of the rock by hand

Machu Picchu

Peruvian high altitude farmers after a hard day's work

Next page: Sunday best

Cusco

Lunch anyone? Roast guinea pigs

You can't stop farmers assessing crops for yield

Matto Grosso cropped as far as the eye could see not much sign of the 20% conservation required by Brazilian law

Nelore cattle brought out for our approval

A farrowing pen in the Matto Grosso. Note the open sides

The ladies were each given a flower

The party that went to Peru and Ecuador

AFRICA

Tanzania

It was an agricultural banker friend on the phone. He had been a great supporter when I launched LEAF (Linking Environment and Farming) a few years previously and he wanted to involve me in a competition his bank was planning. It was aimed at young people and would involve them writing an environment strategy for a typical farm that would be described on the entry form. He was also a supporter of the charity Farm Africa which had been set up to help Africans grow more of their own food and become self-sufficient and he was proposing that the prize for the best strategy would be a trip to Tanzania to visit some Farm Africa projects. The trip would also take in a few days' safari in the Serengeti National Park. Oh, and he would like me to go with the winners as part of the prize.

How could I refuse? Of course, I said yes and we began to reserve dates in the diary. I didn't have to do anything; just join half a dozen interesting young farmers who wrote the best entries in the competition. We gathered at Heathrow then flew off to Arusha Airport that I believe has now been renamed Kilimanjaro Airport because it is close to the mountain so many people want to climb. Indeed, we had a marvellous view of the peak as we came in to land.

We were met by a driver in a long wheelbase Land Rover that was to be our transport for the trip. We piled our luggage in the back and set off. The first few miles around the town were on good black top roads but pretty soon we were on what I would describe as bad farm tracks and then they got worse. At one point we came across a small lorry that had lost one of its front wheels. It had broken off at the axle. There was nothing we could do to help so we carried on, eventually arriving at the village where Farm Africa was working.

We were to stay there for a couple of nights and were shown into our accommodation, which looked a few stars up from the surrounding huts. Ours was a superior looking hut in which were enough camp beds for our party. There was no running water or bathroom facilities. And no private rooms – we all dossed down together. However, we knew we were there to try to help others worse off than ourselves so we did not complain.

A local lady served us supper from a big pot. I think it was goat stew but I'm not sure. And then we decided to have an early night. I'm bound to say I did not sleep well. It was hot and the bed was uncomfortable. Always an early riser, I was up even earlier the next morning and wandered outside to stretch my legs. A stream ran past the hut and a little girl was collecting water in a can, presumably for her family's breakfast. A few yards upstream a cow was defecating into the water. It was the first of many shocks over the next few days.

The Farm Africa representative in charge of helping the people was a local man who had been trained by a white teacher from England. His transport around the several villages he supported was a motorbike which was becoming unreliable. Farm Africa had arranged a new one for him but it was stuck in the port of Dar es Salaam and the port authorities would not release it to him without a bribe. Farm Africa would not pay a bribe, on principle, so the situation was deadlocked. Corruption ruled, OK.

He told us of the reforms he was trying to introduce. The local livestock was mainly goats. And goats will eat almost anything. Traditionally the village goats had been allowed to roam anywhere and had eaten every bit of grass and young trees as they had emerged, which meant they constantly had to roam further for their food and created a widening desert. He was teaching the women (who did most of the work while their husbands drank beer and put the world to rights) to contain their goats in crude sheds and bring feed to them, allowing trees and natural vegetation to re-establish. The second part of the goat project was to supply superior goats from England with much better potential to give milk and then encourage them to breed kids that could be distributed around the village. We met women who were enthusiastic for both aspects of the goat business and it seemed to be working.

But the women themselves had been adding to the problem of desertification when they cut wood to burn on their fires to cook food. Farm Africa had designed a fuel-efficient cooking fire that cooked food using a fraction of the wood and the representative was teaching the ladies how to make them. He was also advocating mixed cropping in their gardens with clovers that took nitrogen from the air alongside maize so that the clover would, in effect, fertilise the maize. Interesting isn't it that similar techniques are currently being looked at on arable farms in the UK.

It seemed to us eminently sensible that these DIY techniques were being taught in the villages. Unlike an American scheme elsewhere in Africa, masterminded by ex-president Jimmy Carter. Apparently they had gone in, with millions of dollars behind them, cleared several villages, ploughed up all their land and planted maize. American drivers had worked the machines and later trained the locals how to use them. Then they walked away and left it to the locals. But these locals had not fully understood how to maintain the machines which, after a while, broke down. And now, the area was littered with broken down tractors in huge fields that produced very little. Furthermore, their village communities had gone. Maybe it was an apocryphal story but it reinforced Farm Africa's approach.

That said, the village we were staying in could have done with some of Jimmy Carter's millions. Fresh tap water would have been a start and the little hospital nearby, we were told, was so full that patients were lying two to a bed. And they were unable to get or afford many drugs so most patients were given aspirin, whatever their problem.

Those few days with Farm Africa were a sharp lesson and I suspect all of us on that visit have thought a lot about it since and done what we could to support its efforts.

And then, not without some feelings of guilt at what we had left behind, we went off on safari. We went first to the Ngorongoro Crater, the world's largest caldera, in other words what was left after the cone of a gigantic volcano had collapsed. It was about 18 kms diameter. We stopped first at the lodge overlooking the crater. Binoculars out and we could see some of the wildlife below us. Then our driver took us down one of the tracks to get nearer to them.

I was amazed at how close we were able to get to lions, wildebeests, jackals and birds and our cameras clicked constantly. The animals were accustomed to vehicles and didn't see them as threats and we were almost ignored by them. I'm not sure what would have happened if we had dismounted. But none of us did more than lean out of the windows and take photographs. Kodak and Fuji did pretty well out of that trip. It was before the days of phone cameras and we could not help trying to capture each new sighting on our Box Brownies. I felt like David Attenborough for a while.

We went closer to the lake at the low point in the crater where thousands of bright pink flamingos stood in the water, occasionally dipping their beaks to search for food. Wildebeests and gazelles wandered by and a warthog emerged from a wallow. Over the other side of the lake a group of hippos lazed in the sun and a secretary bird came and perched on the branch of a half-dead tree. A lone elephant walked into view and then came to have a drink. We were mesmerised. It was one of those moments in life when you feel privileged to be there.

But it was time to move on. We were scheduled to stay for the next few nights in a luxury lodge beside a waterhole in the Serengeti. It was as nice as it sounds and we enjoyed it all the more because of the privations we had endured the past few nights. We slept well on comfortable mattresses.

Next morning we toured the Serengeti. Our driver said he would try to show us the big five, that is lions, leopards, rhinoceros, elephant and buffalo. He also said we were there at a good time – it was early July – to see the wildebeest migration. This is when between one and two million wildebeests accompanied by a few hundred thousand zebras migrate from the Serengeti to the Maasai Mara in search of better grass. They come back in spring after the Serengeti grazing has recovered but, in whichever direction, the movement of these great herds is an incredible sight – and sound because there is a continuous mooing from them as they walk. Or at least the wildebeests' version of mooing. It's actually more like grunting.

Sure enough, we did see the big five that day. The term does not mean they are the biggest, although they are pretty large, but that they are the most dangerous. The easiest to find were the lions. We saw one group of lionesses lazing on a rock without a care in the world.

And we saw a group of three young lions that had been ejected from their pride when they became adults and were living together until they found a pride of their own. They had obviously fed recently and were not hungry and they walked, without hurrying, in single file across the plain alongside a herd of wildebeest, as if they owned the place.

We found elephants and rhinos at waterholes neither disturbing the others and we saw hippos in a pond with just their eyes, noses and backs above the water. But a leopard, which is more of a solitary animal, was more difficult. As we searched, we came across a zebra that had been killed by a big cat of some kind being cleaned up by a flock of vultures with a secretary bird apparently supervising the operation. And we saw giraffes with their ridiculously long but elegant necks eating leaves from high branches in the few trees on the plain and loads of gazelles of various kinds. Then the driver shouted, "Yes! There's our leopard." And there, high in an acacia tree, was a recumbent leopard. It had found a branch strong enough to take its weight and lay there with its front feet and legs either side of the branch. Whether it was asleep or not we could not tell. Probably not because these animals are constantly alert. But it paid no apparent heed to us as we snapped yet more photos.

Back to the lodge after a fascinating day and another good night's sleep. It would soon be time to go home. But as part of the prize for the young farmers I felt I had had a prize myself – a fascinating few days in the village and on the plain.

South Africa

In the autumn of 1991, I attended a conference in London one morning and had arranged a meeting with the Trade Attaché at the High Commission of South Africa in the afternoon. Jill Lewis and I had decided on a tour of South Africa and I wanted to get as many contacts as I could as part of my preparation. There was time between these two appointments for a quick bite and I decided to pop into the Farmers Club in Whitehall Court, where I was a long-term member, for a beer and a sandwich.

I had just ordered it from Rosemary, a lovely Irish woman who served behind the bar and had done it so long she was part of the fixtures and fittings of the club, when two smartly dressed men walked in behind me. I turned to welcome them but before I could say anything one of them said, "Hello, I'm from South Africa. Are you a farmer?" I replied that I was and volunteered that it was a coincidence because I was due at his High Commission in Trafalgar Square in half an hour. "And why are you going to my High Commission?" he asked. So I explained to him that I was in the middle of arranging a fact-finding tour of South Africa to look round farms. "Well, perhaps I can help," he said. "I happen to be the minister of agriculture for South Africa."

He went on to introduce himself properly as Kraai van Niekerk and his colleague and chief of staff, Mr Van De Merwe. It transpired that they were in London to speak to the Ministry of Agriculture about trade between our two countries that had become possible since President F. W. de Klerk abolished apartheid. They had hoped to meet John Gummer, who was UK minister of agriculture at the time, but they had been fobbed off with Baroness Trumpington as Gummer was still not convinced by their bona-fides. I commented that Jean Trumpington, who was a real hoot, would have been more fun than Gummer but that was not the point of their visit.

"So, how do you know these people?" Kraai asked. "I present TV programmes for farmers and I write columns for the *Farmers Weekly* and the *Financial Times*," I admitted, "so I meet them fairly regularly." "Oh really," he said. "I'm so pleased you're coming to South Africa to see for yourself what is happening rather than believe what you are told by the BBC. You know, I can show you more than you will ever see on your tour. Give me your card and I will arrange an additional tour for you and you will be a guest of the South African government." I replied that this was most generous but that I would be travelling with my wife. "That's OK," he said, "she can come too."

At which point I had to leave to keep my contact at the High Commission where I hardly dared to admit that I had just met with his boss. He was very helpful and gave me details of people I should contact and I returned home on the train. I told Lorna about my meeting in the club but I warned her not to get too excited because I had heard such promises from politicians before and they didn't come to anything. But three weeks later a letter arrived from Pretoria to propose a programme and tell me that two of the top people in the South

African Ministry of Agriculture had been assigned to lead myself and my wife on a ten-day tour after I had finished with my own. And the wife of one of these men would accompany us to keep Lorna company.

Suffice to say that my tour went well and we visited some wonderful farms and met some incredible farmers. Some of them had bred their own strains of cattle from original British breeds to suit their own farms and the South African climate. They reminded me of some Scottish farmers I had met who really knew their cattle. But I was most impressed by the way in which some of those farmers' wives looked after the health and welfare of their workers and their families. Yes, the workers lived in rather crude houses by Western standards, but there were large numbers of workers on every farm and every child was found work when he or she was old enough. They seemed to be loyal and part of the family. It distressed me to hear that agitators were actively, even then, trying to turn workers against their employers. And I understand that has become much worse in recent years to the point that farmers are being murdered regularly, despite strict precautions. How sad.

As light relief from all the farming, we went to the Kruger National Game Reserve. This is the biggest in South Africa and probably the most famous. It's about five million acres and it has a fence all around it. We spent an enjoyable day driving round the park on its many black top roads looking at the animals. They were all there. The big five (elephants, lions, rhinoceros, giraffes, leopards, as well as African buffalo) and all their predators and fellow travellers. Although it was sad to see that many of them were in poor condition. The reason was obvious. The area was in the middle of a drought and the grass hadn't grown. That meant the gazelles and the zebras and the wildebeest had grown thin which, in turn meant when the lions and the leopards killed one of them the meal was not as filling as it should have been. In addition, the trees were stunted and short of leaves so that the elephants and the giraffes were hungry too. And because of the fence, none of the animals could escape to find food elsewhere. It made you wonder at the wisdom of the fence.

Late afternoon of that same day – it was a Friday – we went to a peach orchard nearby where they were picking and packing the fruit for export. The managers there were very concerned about the drought. Indeed, they were about to hold their weekly prayer meeting to pray for rain in which the 300 workers would take part. They asked if we would like to take part in the service. Of course, we said yes and we sat on the little hill outside the packhouse as the workers filed out and sat down on the grass. The local pastor was a Scot and he opened the service by introducing a hymn which we all sang. Listening to the wonderful harmonies instinctively sung by the black workers was wonderful.

Then the pastor read a passage from the bible, followed by a prayer in which he asked God for rain. "Now, would anyone else like to share a prayer with us?" he asked and a couple of the workers offered their prayers. Then a third worker stood up and said, "We have some guests from abroad with us and I wonder if one of them would like to join us in prayer?" The pastor looked at me and I felt some hands on my back pushing me forward and I did my best to persuade God to send rain.

Another hymn, and that was the end of the service, and we loaded up into our bus to go and find our hotel just down the road from the peach orchard. It was a nice hotel and I remember Lorna found a tiny frog in the bath. I had a shower to wash the day's dust off before dinner and as I did so there was a crack of thunder and it began to rain, heavily. It only lasted fifteen minutes but ever after that I was known as the rainmaker. Funny though, it never worked during a dry spell on the farm at home.

We crossed the Great Rift Valley, one of the biggest natural features in the world, formed over millions of years and stretching from the Middle East to Mozambique, marking where two of the Earth's plates will one day split Africa. We followed the railway line where the young journalist, Winston Churchill, was captured by the Boers during the Boer War. We stayed at the iconic Mount Nelson Hotel on the lower slopes of Table Mountain in Cape Town and we went up the mountain itself on the cable car. We visited the beautiful city of Pretoria, full of jacaranda trees, and we called in on a farm producing protea flowers which were claimed to be drought resistant and able to regenerate after fire – a symbol of South Africa's resilience, we were told. And we tasted beautiful wines at Stellenbosch, the centre of the wine-growing area of South Africa. It was there that the government people picked up Lorna and me for our extended tour and we left the party to find their own way home.

Our three hosts apologised that they had only been able to get a six-seater car from the government and it didn't have air conditioning. But it was comfortable enough and we could always open the windows. They took us first to a farm where three black farmers had been subsidised by the government to set up a small cooperative to fatten beef cattle. The structure was that a white advisory officer advised a black advisor – whose name was Pencil – who, in turn, advised the three farmers. The theory was that the unsophisticated farmers would respond better to a black advisor than to a white one. On the farm was a small beef lot containing about fifty animals and they looked to be in good condition. Around the lot were fields of maize – the Africans called them mealies – which were destined to be made into silage for zero grazing through the year. For the uninitiated, zero grazing is when the animals have all their food brought to them and do not at any time leave the containment of the beef lot to graze.

We were introduced to the three farmers, one of whom was small in stature but was obviously the leader. "So, are you a farmer?" he asked me. I told him I was and we went on to discuss some of the differences between my farming and his. After a bit of this back and forth he asked, "Do you have baboons in your mealies?" I laughed and said no, that we didn't have that kind of problem, to which he responded, "How do you keep them away?" It was clearly difficult for him to imagine a climate where wild baboons did not exist.

It was March 1992 and Nelson Mandela had been freed from prison on Robben Island two years earlier. President F. W. de Klerk had declared a referendum on whether apartheid should be ended in South Africa and we were in the run-up to that event. Predictably it dominated every conversation and the talk with our government guides was no exception. It was clear that they felt apartheid was dead already and it was time to change.

Meanwhile they took us to other interesting farms where the Ministry had an interest, then to Bloemfontein, and on to Kimberley, the centre of the diamond industry, where a huge volcanic crater dominated everything around it.

It was interesting to learn how thousands of tonnes of volcanic rock are broken and sorted to find one diamond. Also about the stranglehold the Kimberley-based industry has on the number of gems released for sale each year – to keep the price up, obviously. Fortunately I was able to persuade Lorna that we didn't have time to buy any diamonds. And then we traced our way along the Orange River, through what felt and looked like desert until we came to an oasis. It wasn't an oasis, of course. It was a farm on a bend in the river where the farmer had harnessed the water to grow an array of vegetables and salad crops. It was almost like hydroponics with the crops growing in sand and the farmer adding fertiliser and water from the river. The natural heat from the sun completed the combination of needs and the crops looked fantastic. I wondered how, in such an isolated spot, he sold his produce but he assured me that wholesalers would come and get his superior greens and that he was able to charge premium prices.

We were on our way towards Augrabies Falls National Park. The falls consist of water released from the Orange River over the rocks around it and the locals call it the noisy falls. But the surroundings were vast and beautiful, with gigantic rock formations that made you feel small. We were to meet Kraai van Niekerk and his wife, Therese, at their holiday home in the Augrabies and spend the night with them there. When we arrived, Kraai had already fired up the barbecue ready for supper. He took me to his balcony overlooking the magnificent park and said, "This is where I think the world started." I could see what he meant.

There followed an enjoyable evening eating and drinking and talking about what Lorna and I had seen, and about the forthcoming referendum. It lasted into the small hours while we got to know one another better and when our eyes began to droop. Next morning we were to visit Uppington where there was an agricultural show and Kraai was to address a meeting about the referendum. From now on, Lorna and I travelled in the back of Kraai's air-conditioned Mercedes with Kraai driving and Therese in the front passenger seat. Our guides followed in the six-seater. The roads weren't very good. In some cases they were only tracks and Therese told Kraai he was driving too fast on numerous occasions. "The trouble is he thinks he's Jody Scheckter," she said to us in the rear.

We reached Uppington – which, incidentally, was the centre of Kraai's parliamentary constituency – and went straight to the show. It wasn't much, to be honest. It consisted of several pens of fat tailed sheep and a few merinos. The fat tails, we were told, held reserves of fat and moisture to carry the animals over periods of extreme drought as experienced in the nearby Kalahari Desert. The merinos with their heavy wool seemed on the face of it to be unsuited to desert conditions but the locals knew best.

Kraai was next scheduled to speak in the local church hall to a gathering of local people and Lorna and I were invited. We sat at the back, rather self-consciously, because most of the meeting was conducted in Afrikaans, apart from the bit when Kraai introduced us to the crowd. Kraai and Therese pressed the flesh and chatted to people after the meeting then collected us to join our guides. We all stayed in town that night because Kraai's house on his farm had been burned down a few weeks before. It had been planned that we should stay there but disgruntled black people had decided they didn't like a white MP representing them and upset the plan.

Next day we visited that farm and saw the destruction of what had been a beautiful thatched farmhouse. It was the first time they had seen it since the fire. Kraai was fairly sanguine about it but Therese was distraught. They didn't know whether to rebuild in case the same happened again. One of the penalties of being in politics in South Africa. "Let's go and find the sheep," said Kraai to change the subject.

His farm was 32,000 acres of desert. The average rainfall was six inches per year and the average annual temperature was 40°C. He knew the sheep would be close to one of the waterholes on the property but he didn't know which one. It took us two hours to find the flock – 1,300 merinos – which was all the 32,000 acres would support. It wasn't the kind of farming I was used to but fascinating all the same. The sheep were overseen by a neighbouring farmer while Kraai was busy in parliament. But he admitted they wouldn't make him a living, which was one reason he had gone into politics.

Soon after that, our guides – now friends – delivered us back to Johannesburg airport and we flew home. It had been a privileged few days and we did appreciate it. And all because I called at the Farmers Club for a sandwich.

A couple of years later when Mandela had been installed as president of South Africa, Kraai was one of the few white MPs he chose to stay in the Cabinet. He phoned one day and said he and Therese had been invited to attend a Commonwealth Conference in London. The Conference ended on a Friday and they had the weekend free. Could they come and stay with us. Of course, I said yes but I asked him if they would like to have a restful weekend or visit a couple of farms. "You know me by now David. Let's do a bit of farming."

So I arranged for us to visit a Norfolk farm I was overseeing on behalf of Sentry Farming, of which I was a director, on the Saturday. Then on the Sunday to have a pub lunch at Woodbastwick, where he would be able to see some British White cattle belonging to the Cator family and move on to Holkham Hall where my friend Eddie Leicester – more formally titled the Earl of Leicester (apologies for the name dropping) – would show us a small part of his 25,000-acre estate and give us tea. Eddie was particularly pleased to welcome the van Niekerks because he was born in South Africa and had inherited the estate via his uncle. But he had fond memories of his youth in South Africa and was keen to catch up with what was happening there.

As indeed was I. Back home, I asked Kraai what Mandela was like as a president. "Frankly, he is a remarkable man," he said. "He doesn't appear to hold a grudge that we kept him locked up all those years. And he has a knack of finding a compromise that all can support. For instance, sometimes when we sit round the Cabinet table we reach an impasse between us whites and the blacks on the other side of the table. Someone will say we had better call in Madiba (Mandela's nickname). So he comes into the room and he says now, what's the problem and within a few minutes he will come up with a solution that we can all accept. Maybe it's just the force of his personality."

While he was in power, Mandela kept the peace but his successors have not had that same character or force of personality to maintain what he started. Stories coming out of South Africa today tell of farmers being murdered almost weekly. And the economy isn't doing very well either. The country needs another Mandela, but there does not appear to be one around.

I took another party to South Africa a few years after that first trip. We went to similar places as the first one and it didn't include an extension for Lorna and me. But it did include a journey across the Karoo, an area of semi-desert land where you wonder how anyone can survive. In fact, we stayed in one place where the farmers were very stressed and they asked us to join them in one of their houses one evening as they discussed how they could work their way through their lack of profitability. One of their friends had committed suicide a few weeks earlier and it had panicked some of the wives that their husbands might do the same.

Most of them seemed reliant on the production of fibre from angora goats – the only livestock that could live off the sparse grazing in the area. They had set up a factory of sorts to make it into superior pillows and duvets. They were really nice but expensive so limiting the market for them. It was no good telling them to diversify further because not much else could live there. Tourism was one possibility but farmers tours like ours were few and far between. People who want sun and scenery wouldn't be too satisfied with the area which, as one member of our party remarked, was "miles and miles of bugger all". I don't think we were able to help them very much. But remarkably they were helping to educate local children, the offspring of their workers.

There was a school in the area to which black children walked. The trouble was that many had to walk two hours or more from their homes, morning and night. In conjunction with the teachers and the parents it had been agreed that it would be best if the children stayed at school most nights and just walked home at the weekend. This meant finding beds for the children to sleep on and food for them to eat during the week. The farmers' wives we had been speaking to had undertaken to provide these and the school was improving almost weekly.

Before we left the area we went to that school. They had been warned we were coming and we were met by a road full of children singing a welcome to us. The teachers told us that the children's enthusiasm for learning was off the scale, and now that they didn't have to walk to school every day their energy to learn had increased. We thought of the problems in education back home and the truancy and most of us shed a discrete tear. And we dipped our hands in our pockets to add a little to school funds. It was a thought-provoking and inspiring morning.

An acacia tree at sunset in the Serengeti

Flamingos, Wilderbeast and Gazelle in the Ngorongoro crater

Flamingos in the Ngorongoro crater

Male Lions with no pride

Each Zebra has unique markings, like human fingerprints

Secretary bird supervising the feast of Vultures

Female lions relax

Buffalo and Zebra in the Ngorongoro crater

Inquisitive Giraffe

We were met by the whole school on the road singing us a welcome.

A lone elephant in the Ngorongoro crater

A basic schoolroom

A goat compound to Farm Africa's design

Double cropping as advocated by Farm Africa

Milking time

One of the ladies keeping goats

We visited a crocodile farm

Hippopotamus

Zimbabwe and Zambia

On that occasion we went on from South Africa to Zimbabwe, formerly known as Southern Rhodesia. We started in Harare, the capital, and had lunch in the Harare Club, which has a reciprocal arrangement with the Farmers Club in London, before going off with our farmer hosts for the next few days. Whenever possible on these tours I liked to stay with local people. That way you got to know more about the country and the way of life. And Zimbabwean farmers were among the most welcoming. Lorna and I stayed with one of the leaders of Zimbabwean farmers and his wife. He had a loud voice and a commanding manner and we nicknamed him 'Stormin Norman'.

They were a lovely family, with Norman dealing with the crops, and his wife a herd of pigs. She also took care of the workers' health and safety and took them or their wives to hospital when necessary. The farm grew beans, tobacco and maize. While we were there it was necessary to spray the beans with insecticide and I was rather concerned when I saw the operation. The workers were kitted out with plastic overalls but were spraying the insecticide on the crop with handheld sprayers pumping with one hand and holding the spray nozzle in front of them. But they had bare legs and no protection over their mouths. What could I say, except that it would be illegal at home.

That said, we found Zimbabwean agriculture efficient. Norman told us that the climate in Zimbabwe was more reliable than in South Africa which was more subject to droughts. "Many times, our produce has rescued South Africa from famine," he claimed. But he was concerned that with Mugabe as president and the state-sponsored civil unrest affecting farms, that this would not continue. Some farms had already been taken over by militant blacks, with government ministers installed as owners. They had no idea how to farm and the land was lying idle. Inflation was getting worse and there was a great deal of corruption at government level.

"It's getting almost as bad as it was before Mugabe took over," he said and he went on to describe how groups of farmers used to patrol their borders at night to prevent invasion by the militants. Since then, my sources have told me that the situation has got much worse and although Mugabe has been replaced by President Mnangagwa, there has been no improvement. Inflation is out of control and the country that was so productive has descended into chaos.

But back then in the mid 1900s we felt safe and enjoyed the hospitality of the farmers who may have been worried about the future but didn't let it spoil their way of life. And there was no denying that they lived in some style. Big houses with high ceilings and lots of servants to wait on them hand and foot. They'd had it good and they knew it. One day we went with Norman to the country club where a cricket match was in progress. We met many of the farmers in the area and they were pleased to see us. But their main topic of conversation was the government. I sometimes wonder if that club still exists.

Meanwhile we visited some fascinating farms. One crop that was new to me was tobacco. The farmer explained to us how important it was to harvest the tobacco leaves at exactly the right time so that they had no marks or signs of disease on them. And he showed us how the leaves are bunched together and hung in drying sheds to cure before being sent off to the tobacco auction. I gave up smoking when I was twenty-five so it was not of direct interest to me. But as a farmer, growing and marketing crops, I found it very interesting indeed.

We saw Victoria Falls, 'the smoke that thunders', plunging into the Batoka Gorge, we marvelled at its permanent rainbow and we walked through the endless spray. We went to farms growing pineapples and peanuts and raising more wonderful cattle. They were looked after by black herdsmen on horseback and they carefully drove a selection of animals closer to us for inspection. And we went to another school. The pupils were impressively well behaved and the teachers were clearly devoted to their jobs. But we learned the depressing statistic that almost half of the pupils were orphans. It was during the worldwide Aids epidemic and they had lost their parents from that disease. Our farmer hosts were doing their best to support the children of parents they used to employ but they were fighting a losing battle.

I came across a similar problem at the next farm where Lorna and I stayed. The owner had set up a business growing green beans for Marks & Spencer and Sainsbury's. He grew them to a timetable so that he could supply most months of the year and then he packed them according to how his customers demanded. His packing shed was immaculate and every woman had an identical uniform to her neighbour. They trimmed the beans to the appropriate length, then weighed them before packing them in sealable plastic bags ready to place on the UK supermarket shelves. The set-up was at least as good as any food packing unit I had been into at home and probably better than some.

I congratulated the farmer on what he had achieved and asked what his greatest problem was, thinking it might be flying his produce from Harare to Gatwick every night. But that wasn't it. "My biggest problem," he said, "is management. I've got some really good men on this farm and in the packhouse and I'd like to promote them to relieve me of some work. But when I've tried it and paid them more money as befits the extra responsibility, they go straight down to the town, spend it on a prostitute or two, catch Aids and within a year they're dead. Promotion means condemning someone to death and I don't know the answer."

It was a sad note on which to end a memorable tour, but we had heard, on our travels, that several Zimbabwean farmers had already sold up and moved to Zambia where there was a more liberal regime. Zambia used to be called Northern Rhodesia, of course, and it was the next-door country. I resolved to take a tour there when possible because I thought it might have some of the advantages of Zimbabwe without such a corrupt government.

A year or two later, it happened. We were met at Lusaka airport by Daphne who, with her husband, was one of the people to move over from Zimbabwe. She was now the Zambian equivalent of Jill Lewis and had been involved with arranging our tour of Zimbabwe a few years earlier. So she was already a friend and knew the kinds of things we wanted to see.

One of the notable things about Zambia is that it has much better land than Zimbabwe and also an abundance of water for irrigation. The farmers we met were more relaxed about their incomes and security. They were concerned, however, about Chinese investment in the country. Apparently large acreages of some of the best land had been acquired by the Chinese. They weren't sure but they thought it must be the Chinese government that had put up the money and they further assumed it was to grow crops to feed Chinese people in China. In other words, that the produce would be sent to China without ever being offered on local or world markets. I had heard rumours of similar deals being done in other countries so I wasn't surprised.

We stayed in a riverside hotel that was built over the water with raised walkways connecting the rooms. It was open to the river so fish and other water creatures could swim under the rooms and the planks. We thought it was a great novelty until a hippopotamus decided it might be a nice place to spend the night and came in under the rooms in which we were sleeping. I didn't mind until he/she, I don't know which, started to snore, or whatever hippos do when they sleep. It made for a rather disturbed night.

For a 'treat' one day, Daphne had arranged for us to be punted across the Zambezi River. It sounded like fun and we arrived at the riverside in our bus in a good mood. A lady behind a crude desk said, "Sign this please," so we all signed without bothering to read it. We were looking forward to the ride across the river too much. After a little while we climbed into two-person kayaks, every kayak with a man standing on the back with a pole, and were handed a glass of champagne each.

Lorna was in the front of ours, and I was at the back. There seemed to be a slight delay and then we realised why. A motorboat with two men with rifles in the back was going to escort us across. Even then I don't think any of us realised the significance of the armed escort; perhaps it was the champagne, but off we set at a leisurely pace, with all the punters singing a traditional song as they punted us into mid-stream.

The Zambezi is a big river, perhaps a couple of hundred metres across. Suddenly one of the chaps in the motorboat shouted "Hippo!" and the relaxed atmosphere changed to one of panic. The punter men galvanised themselves, and instead of gently floating, our kayaks were pushed along fast enough to pull someone water skiing. That was when we saw a small tidal wave as the hippo raced towards us on the riverbed. The men with the rifles raised them ready to shoot if necessary. At what seemed like the last few seconds before disaster, the hippo swerved and climbed up a bank out of the river, by which time we, in our kayaks, were almost at the other bank.

We disembarked, still in a good mood, and Daphne was there with a cup of coffee to calm us. Just then one of the gunmen passed by and I heard him say to a colleague, "That was a bit of luck." To which I asked, "What do you mean?" "Oh, it's just that we lost a man to a hippo last week. We wouldn't want it to happen two weeks running." Only then did we realise what the papers we had signed were. They indemnified the boat company in case we'd been killed.

I placed these rams in the following order ...

Tobacco being prepared to hang up to dry

The night we sat and heard about a neighbour's suicide and the concerns that others might do it too.
Serious stuff.

Orphaned school children. Their parents died of AIDS.

Tobacco drying

The herdsmen gently steered a bull towards us to inspect

Angora goats

Green beans being packed for UK supermarkets

Flowers being prepared to send to the Dutch clock auction

Victoria Falls with its ever present rainbow in the cloud of spray

AUSTRALIA AND NEW ZEALAND

We flew to Sydney in time for the Royal Sydney Easter Show. It's held every year at Easter time and these days takes place in the arena that was built to accommodate the Sydney Summer Olympics in 2000. No agricultural showground in the world has better facilities. The grand ring is what used to be the athletics arena and the grandstand provides a fantastic viewing platform to see the cattle parades. Because of its proximity to Sydney, it's developed into a fairground as well as a farm show. And although there is stiff competition between cattle and sheep breeders, who regard it as their event, for top honours, there is no doubt it is also designed to attract city people and their children.

The show runs for two weeks and in 2023 attracted some 870,000 visitors. That attendance is not to be sniffed at, and it allows the management to put on a superb event that provides a shop window for Australian farm produce. But when we were there, not long after it moved to the Olympic stadium, about a million were claimed to pass through the turnstiles over the two-week run.

Our party was treated like royalty when we arrived. At least some Australians respect the 'Old Country'. Lunch with the president was the first treat although we were underdressed for such a grand occasion having dressed down for a holiday. But no one seemed to mind and we were pleased to meet some familiar faces of people who had moved to Australia after they got fed up with England. Seats in the grandstand were next and we enjoyed the parade of fine cattle. Lorna and I decided not to ride the helter-skelter or the Ferris wheel but we did enjoy seeing the display of fruit and vegetables arranged by the ladies of the Australian Farmers Union. It was a great day and I left jealous of the facilities and the size of the crowd. I was, at the time, chairman of the organising committee of the Royal Norfolk Show and I would have loved to import some of them.

We stayed in a really nice hotel on The Rocks, in the shadow of Sydney Harbour Bridge. It was so convenient for the opera house and the harbour with loads of eateries and shops nearby. We went in the other direction one afternoon and discovered, in a small square, a man with a guitar singing Australian folk songs – about things like red-backed spiders on the toilet seat, and so on. We loved it and sat and listened to him for ages. We went to Bondi Beach and were disappointed at how small it was. My vision of it previously was of miles and miles of luxurious sand, whereas in reality it's only a few hundred yards wide and is surrounded by shops, AirBnBs and offices.

We took a look at Canberra, the capital of Australia. A city devoted to government, it had a look of order and symmetry. I particularly liked the parliament building set into a small hill and with a roof growing grass. I don't know what rubbish went on inside, but the building they did it in was OK. We also went to the ANZAC memorial high on a hill above Canberra. Viewing the displays of how Australian and New Zealand troops helped win the Second World War, and paid a heavy price in lives, was a quiet inspiration and something we Brits should all be exposed to.

Then it was time to leave the cities and explore the countryside. We were taken to a mountain range in New South Wales called the Warrumbungles which I thought must have been what the Aborigines called it. But I was wrong. They called it 'the crooked mountain' which was rather boring in comparison. The place was crawling, or should I say jumping, with kangaroos that almost posed for our cameras, they were so used to visitors.

The tourist bit over, we headed for a town called Dubbo where we were to meet our hosts for the next few days. Arthur Borrill from north Lincolnshire, and Lorna and I went with the Whites, with whom we stayed for the next few nights. They had a young son and a startlingly beautiful daughter called Sonia who was the reigning beauty queen of the nearby town of Tamworth. But her good looks didn't stop her mucking in on the farm. She did, however, have a pet kangaroo called Joey. Sonia came to stay with us in England for several months the following year, and the cars and pickups of the Norfolk beaus wore ruts in our drive.

The Whites' farm grew maize and sorghum among other things and was plagued by a flock of noisy galahs, pink-breasted parrot-like birds that feed off such crops and cause farmers problems. A bit like wood pigeons in Britain, only much prettier. So the boss was constantly preoccupied with frightening them off his crops. But Jill White took us to a nearby farm where they were mining cat litter. This was a naturally occurring seam of a silicon-type substance that they were digging out of the subsoil, bagging and selling to pet shops. The farmer had discovered it accidentally, and it was making him a fortune, apparently. The best possible type of diversification.

The first night we were there we talked long into the night about farming, and people we all knew, and local snakes which were poisonous. We hadn't really got our bearings of the house. It was very hot and there were nets over most of the doors to let what breeze there was pass through. And it was an extensive bungalow. Lorna had to get up in the middle of the night to go to the toilet but couldn't remember where the lavatory was. In desperation she decided to go outside on the lawn but as she was 'performing' she remembered the talk of snakes and, panicking, rushed back into the house.

She admitted this at breakfast and it caused some amusement, particularly when the Whites admitted they had been awake during the entire episode but thought they didn't know us well enough to intervene. That's one way to get to know people.

We carried on north into Queensland seeing fields of cotton being flood irrigated, and sugar cane grown on a massive scale. It made me realise again just how much competition there was for the sweet teeth of the world's consumers. And this was fully mechanised. A brief stop in Brisbane, then off for a weekend in a gorgeous beachfront hotel at the north end of the 40-mile beach. It wasn't 40 miles as we found when our friend, Alan Alston, Lorna and I hired a 4wd vehicle and drove along it. But we had to find our way through rainforest to get to the beach and nearly got stuck on some prominent roots. But it was a pleasant drive beside the Pacific and we made it safely back to the hotel.

Then we flew to Perth. Okay, we missed out the middle of the country but I wanted to visit some friends who lived there and see the contrast with New South Wales and Queensland. And we did the middle a few years later, as I will explain.

To imagine the size of Western Australia consider this; Perth, which is its capital, is as far from its northern border as London is from Moscow.

I had made an appointment to interview the Minister of agriculture for Western Australia, Ernie Bridge, who was an Aboriginal. His secretary had told me he could only spare half an hour so I was ready with my questions.

He greeted me warmly and we started talking. He had invited two of his civil servants to join us and we had an animated conversation for nearly two hours. Clearly his diary was flexible if he was enjoying himself.

During our discussion we talked about water and the fact that both the UK government and the Australian government were in the middle of imposing restrictions on nitrogen fertiliser use on crops. "It's an absolute nonsense," he said. "When I was a little boy on the sheep station I used to dig a hole in the ground until I found water, leave it to settle for a bit, then scoop it up into my mouth and drink it. It never did me any harm." To which one of his civil servants commented, "Well, it turned your skin black." He obviously had a relaxed relationship with his civil servants, perhaps because before getting into politics he'd been a folk singer and he gave me a signed photograph of himself strumming a guitar.

In Perth we stayed in an enormous hotel that doubled as a casino. It was about ten storeys high, built in the shape of a C with the open end being the entrance and reception. The middle was open and every room had a balcony looking down onto the floor where the casino operated. I had no idea that gambling was so popular in Australia, although observing those who participated, from the balcony outside our room, it appeared that a high proportion were Japanese. This demographic of the crowd did coincide with stories I'd heard that the Japanese were buying up large chunks of Australia, and although I never found out who owned the hotel, I would not have been surprised if they were Japanese.

We wanted to visit some friends who had moved out from Britain a few years earlier. So, we hired a car and drove to their farm. It was about a hundred miles east of Perth, or as Colin had described it to me, "a three tin trip." In other words, in the heat of Western Australia you needed to take three tins of lager to drink along the way.

We arrived and were greeted with a warm welcome. But all was not well financially. Ian, Colin's son, had had a nearly total crop failure with his wheat the year before, and by the look of his fields he could expect another after we left. To make ends meet, Ian had taken a job as a lorry driver for mining companies further north, leaving his wife and children to look after the farm.

It wasn't what they wanted, nor what they expected when they moved to Australia but the climate there is unforgiving and their experience had been shared by all their neighbours. "You might get good rains and decent crops one year in five," Ian said, "and that's what you have to expect." But they were not sorry they had taken the plunge and moved out there. Their children were enjoying life on the farm and developing a real sense of responsibility. Anne was a bit lonely at times but Ian was able to get home fairly regularly when his routes passed near the farm. I suppose you develop self-preservation instincts when you live in such a climate. But I'm not sure I could do it.

We drove south of Perth to Margaret River, the centre of a brewing and wine-growing industry that appeared to be prospering despite the drought. And, of course, we had another wine tasting. It was there that I learned that many wines are stored in oak barrels that are burned before use. I remember it well because we were offered some Sauvignon Blanc that had been stored in burned oak casks and I thought it was awful. I have tried to avoid such wines ever since.

Some years later I commented to Carolyne Cree at Field Farm Tours that although I had 'done' Australia east to west, I wouldn't mind doing it north to south. So, in the year 2000 I led a party that started in Darwin and progressed south. The year was significant because a few days before we were scheduled to depart, foot-and-mouth disease was confirmed in Britain. For a few days there was a doubt as to whether we would be allowed into Australia but the authorities relented and we set off.

We arrived at Darwin airport at about three in the morning. It wasn't very sociable and we expected the place to be deserted. How wrong we were. Knowledge of our visit had preceded us and we were met by the full force of border controls. They knew we were farmers and acted in the interests of Australian farmers. All of our cases were opened and checked and there were about four dogs sniffing them as well. You'd think we were a pop group on drugs.

One of the border officers came to me and apologised for how long all their checks were taking at this time of night. "But we cannot afford to get foot-and-mouth in Australia," he said. I replied that we fully appreciated the care they were taking and that we wished our border officers would take as much trouble to prevent diseases getting into Britain.

One of the first visits we made was to a comprehensive irrigation system installed for the farmers in this hot region of the country. It was impressive and the locals enthused about how effective it was. We took a boat down the river to see how the water was being harnessed and passed a crocodile sunning itself on a riverbank. We also passed a flock, if that's the right description of them, of enormous bats, otherwise known as flying foxes, hanging upside down from the branches of riverside trees. They were a few hundred yards away but you could smell them from the boat.

Then we went to a crocodile farm where they were breeding them for their skins. Ladies like the patterns on their shoes and handbags, apparently, and this farm was geared up to respond to that demand. They were about to take a batch of newly hatched eggs out of the incubator and we were invited to see the newborn crocs. A man pulled the drawer out of the machine and brought it to us on the steps of his office. They were lively little critters and a few of them escaped as we were taking photographs. One of our party picked one up to put back in the tray and got bitten quite sharply on his finger. They were only minutes old but they already knew how to attack.

That evening we were invited to a local bar that we were told was really special. The bar itself was a plank of wood held up by two 40-gallon oil drums. The barman wore a hat full of corks and the drinks were on what looked like a workshop bench. The till appeared to be a dried testicle bag that any bull would have been proud of – if he were still alive. In other words, you would not have been surprised if Crocodile Dundee himself had walked in. But the beer was good and cold. It went down a treat in that heat.

Next stop Ayers Rock, or Uluru as it's now called since the Aborigines claimed it as a holy place from their heritage. It is, as many photographs prove, a great big lump of stone in an otherwise bare landscape. But it attracts large crowds to see it change colour as the sun goes down. In fact, the rock doesn't change but the sun does and this is reflected onto the rock. Or have I spoiled the illusion? In any case, we stood there and watched it with the rest.

We were booked in at a smart hotel nearby and served the hottest curry dish for dinner that I have ever had in my mouth. My lips were burning for hours afterwards. But the rooms were pretty good and Lorna and I slept well. But next morning we found that one of our number was shouting at the receptionist demanding a refund. I thought I had better try and sort out the problem, and asked him what the problem was. I should add that it was the same man who had been left behind in Brazil because he was talking to his girlfriend on the phone. It transpired that his current girlfriend had given him a heart-shaped chocolate before he left for our tour, that he had laid it on his bedside table before going to sleep only to find that mice had eaten most of it during the night.

I tried not to laugh as the poor receptionist explained that they had a plague of desert mice and that one of them must have come in under his door. She offered him more chocolate but that made him even more angry. After that I left him to it. I'm not sure whether he got a refund or not. We were moving on anyway.

We headed for Adelaide, and a visit to a dairy farm run by a Suffolk family who had moved out to Australia several years earlier. They appeared to be doing well. They relied heavily on grass, and the rain was more reliable there than in many other areas of the country. They were milking several hundred cows and gave the impression that the price they were getting for milk was satisfactory. Back home, dairy farmers were struggling with ever lower prices from milk processing companies, so that was an eye-opener.

Back on the bus, we went along the coast road towards Melbourne pausing to look at the Apostles on the way. These are a group of twelve limestone rocks, or stacks, in the sea off Port Campbell National Park that have become a tourist attraction. Melbourne was a pleasant city which we enjoyed, briefly, before crossing to Tasmania.

We loved Tasmania. I had always thought it was a bit like the Isle of Wight to England – three or four miles away. But it's much further from Australia than that – nearly 200 miles. And it's much bigger than I thought as well – about half the size of England. Driving round the island was a bit like driving around Scotland. The scenery was similar and the lack of traffic too. We called at a vineyard – yes, another one – named after one of the Tolpuddle Martyrs, George Loveless, because he worked on the farm for a while after he was released from the nearby penal colony at Port Arthur, to which he was deported for trying to start a trade union. Although what Loveless would have thought of his name being associated with a farm now producing wine, given his Methodist belief about the evils of strong drink, I don't know.

We went to Port Arthur and walked round the prison cells that were, as you might expect, small and dark and they must have been dreadful for the inmates. But Port Arthur itself was a pleasant little bay of the kind you might seek out for a camping holiday. I don't know how much time the prisoners were allowed out of their cells, but that time must have been rather pleasant.

And so ended our second tour of Australia. We didn't see it all by any means, but what we did see we enjoyed, particularly the people, who were friendly and welcoming. Most of them had badly behaved ancestors anyway so they may well have been our distant cousins.

In 1985 New Zealand did away with farm subsidies. The country was in trouble economically. It had received two shocks in the previous few years when Britain joined the EEC and stopped buying as many New Zealand lambs, or as much butter, and OPEC tripled the price of oil. The New Zealand government decided that the only way out of their problems was to stop guaranteeing farm prices and let the market decide what farmers got for their produce. As one New Zealand politician put it to me, "We realised that three and a half million people couldn't afford to subsidise seventy million sheep." Until 1985, New Zealand had guaranteed farm prices, just as almost every other country had in some way or another. It was done to ensure food security and as an insurance against bad weather.

But New Zealand felt it had no alternative. With such a small population, and an economy based on agriculture, the policy was bleeding the people dry. And so the momentous decision was made. It was clear that it would cause hardship to many farmers in the short term so the government guaranteed all current farm debt. It also made borrowing cheaper and easier to arrange. It hoped that the undoubted advantages of climate that New Zealand agriculture enjoyed, and already established markets for its produce, would enable the most efficient farmers to survive.

I watched all this from the UK and thought I had better go there and see for myself. Another phone call to Jill Lewis was made and we started making plans to do a tour of New Zealand. Fortunately, other farmers in the UK felt they too should be informed about what was happening over there and we soon gathered a party together. We flew into Auckland, arriving in the evening, local time, and there was a message for me at the hotel from the New Zealand Broadcasting Corporation – please would I go to the Auckland studio at 7.30 the next morning to be interviewed by the presenter.

Who had told the programme that I was coming I don't know, but I thought I had better go, and ordered a taxi for the next morning. When I got there I was almost immediately ushered into the studio to be confronted by an interviewer who attacked me, verbally, for the fact that Britain and Europe were still paying farm subsidies whereas New Zealand wasn't. I tried to explain that I did not control policies, but he said, "You receive subsidies, don't you?" I admitted that I did but again had to defend myself against his accusations. I remember saying that it would not be reasonable for me to refuse subsidies while all around me were getting them. With that he thanked me and turned to the next item in his running order.

I was rather sorry I had accepted the invitation because I was on the defensive most of the time and that is not a good place to be. But what was done was done and I hoped that the farmers we were going to see had not heard my dismal performance. In the event I don't think they did. Or if so, they didn't mention it. Although we did get quite a lot of stick from some farmers as we went along, that we were "living off the state".

We travelled around the North Island first. Geologically it is actively volcanic whereas the South Island was carved by southern ice ages. We visited dairy farms with hundreds of cows, which was unusual to us from the UK at the time. The cows had half their tails cut off so as not to swipe them round onto the people milking them. They were grazing on almost pure clover swards which are rich in protein but cause flatulence, and that can be fatal to cows. So, each time a cow came into the milking parlour there was a student ready with a bottle of indigestion medicine. The cows were so used to it that they put their heads up to receive it when they were in position. The other thing about the cows was that they were small, the result of breeding them for the first time when they were only about eighteen months old, about half the age we were breeding them in the UK at the time.

In other words, the average dairy herd in New Zealand was not the idyllic small herd of Jersey cows grazing in acres of lush grass as advertised on TV when the New Zealand Dairy Board wanted to sell butter. The reality was of crowds of short-tailed Friesians gasping for indigestion medicine and being treated like machines, rather than animals. This was the result of intense market forces and lack of animal welfare regulations. You could argue that New Zealand farmers had been forced to intensify to this extent by its government's policies. Whether the situation has improved since, I don't really know because I haven't been back. But if it hasn't improved it should have.

We went to Lake Taupo where I was scheduled to see an old friend who used to be the estate manager for Lord Beaverbrook during the Second World War. His influence behind the scenes was probably the basis of Beaverbrook's support for British agriculture. He owned the *Daily Express*, and that paper was consistently supportive of farmers, presumably on the instructions of its owner. My friend, who was a New Zealander, had retired to a bungalow overlooking Lake Taupo. A lovely spot and it was good to see him again.

The freshwater lake is the biggest in New Zealand and was left after a huge volcanic eruption thousands of years ago. Our guide suggested a boat ride on the lake and we split up and chose a few with fishing rods on board. I don't claim to be a fisherman but when it came to my turn, rainbow trout seemed to want to be caught. I got five in the space of half an hour, and it was a good feeling. A few miles north of Taupo, we went to Huka Falls and witnessed geothermal activity similar to what I had seen in Yellowstone Park and much later in Iceland. Whether Huka was the origin of the trademark performance of the New Zealand rugby team I never found out. But it certainly came from the Māori language.

We found our way to Wellington, ready to cross to the South Island, but before we left, we had dinner on a boat in the bay. It was very nice, but the boat went round in circles to avoid rough waves, and, cynic that I am, I wondered whether it was worth the effort. But perhaps I was still feeling upset by the radio interview and the belching cows.

Next day we were on the ferry to Blenheim on the South Island and then a glorious ride over the Canterbury Plains to Christchurch. By the time we were there, the seventy million sheep had been almost halved in number, and the Plains were a trifle under grazed we thought, but we began to see evidence of alternative livestock enterprises that had sprung up after the policy change; angora goats were one of the main kinds of livestock that had been newly introduced to produce fibre for upmarket fashion. They were the same as we had seen in South Africa and we wondered if the market might be becoming overstocked and the price might come down. But the New Zealanders we met were still enthusiastic for this new line so we did not think it right to disabuse them.

On arable farms there had been an upsurge in avocados and kiwi fruit. These would be sold to European markets at premium prices, the farmer's hoped. But they had to watch out for transport costs in the way that they didn't have to with lamb because it was frozen. Speaking of lamb, we went to a slaughterhouse specialising in lamb and saw how they were responding to any market they could find. The Muslim market demands animals are slaughtered according to halal rules, of course, and we saw an imam sitting beside the hooks on which the lambs were being brought towards him wielding a long knife and saying a prayer over every lamb he stabbed in the throat. He was covered in blood and was obviously content to be doing it. But it didn't go down well with the ladies in our group. When one or two mentioned the fact, the guide said, "If that's what the market wants, that's what it gets." And he went on to say there was another department that might upset them even more. Having said it, he immediately regretted it, and said he should not have opened his mouth. Lorna said to him that he had to show it to them now. So, he took them to a room where girls were stripping out the lambs' intestines and washing them. "Are these for sausage skins?" Lorna asked. "No, they're made into condoms for people whose religion doesn't allow them to use rubber." You learn something new every day.

We went on towards Dunedin, named after Edinburgh in recognition of where some of the first European settlers came from, and on the way passed a queue of people waiting to bungee jump down a gorge into a river running beneath a bridge. I asked if any of our group wanted to have a go but got no takers. So we pressed on.

There is a line of mountains running the whole length of the South Island and the scenery is impressive. The highest of the mountains in this range is Mount Cook, which is the centre of an active winter sports industry. We took a side trip to view it from afar but it was not the winter sports season. Though we could still see the snow on the upper slopes.

And then to Gore. This was the arable area of the South Island, and Lorna had a distant relative farming there. Her cousin, Margaret, had married Graham Solari of the Shropshire farming family, and one of his brothers had gone out to New Zealand to farm. I had made contact with him through the family and by prearrangement, the whole group turned up in his yard. It was immediately obvious that he was a good farmer growing wheat and barley and peas – much like we were at home. And his crops looked excellent.

He explained that his soil was volcanic and the climate in the area was ideal for his kind of farming. A few years after we were there he was named as having grown the world record yield of wheat – something over 15 tonnes per hectare – and was in the Guinness Book of Records for his achievement.

That record has been broken a few times since, again by New Zealanders and I believe it now stands at over 17 tonnes per hectare, this time held by a Lincolnshire farmer on the best silt land there – in other words, twice the average yield in the UK. But the fact that the record has been broken several times by New Zealand farmers confirms that they have climatic advantages over most other parts of the world. That's why they have survived world markets without subsidies while others have been forced out of business.

The party that went to Australia

Sonia White - beauty queen of Tamworth

Ernie Bridge, the minister of agriculture for Western Australia who was an Aboriginal.

Some of the "Apostles"

Cows on the farm of a man who used to live in Suffolk

The arena at the Royal Sydney Show

One of the farmers' exhibits at the royal Sydney Show

Merinos for inspection

SNIPPETS

I could go on.

I counted recently and realised that I've visited a couple of dozen other countries, as well as those already mentioned, for radio, for TV, for Field Farm Tours, or for holidays. I've been very lucky and I am the first to admit it. But I don't want to fall into the trap that some do, of boring others with their holiday snaps. So, to end with I'll pick out a few notable incidents that have stuck in my mind which may raise a smile or even an eyebrow.

I went with an Anglia TV crew to Spain. It was just before that country entered the EU and we wanted to see how their agriculture might fare under the new regime. Our researcher, David Sawday, had gone on ahead and found a larger-than-life farmer who he thought would be a suitable subject to feature on our programme. His name was Leopold Il Conde de la Maza, Poli to his friends. 'Conde' means 'count', by the way, so he was a Spanish aristocrat. More than that, he was the mayor of his local town, Morón de la Frontera, and he rode a motorbike to work in the town every day. He had an imposing appearance. His height was at least 6ft 3in. He had broad shoulders and quite a wide waist. He also had a glass eye as a result of a bull fighting incident many years previously.

And that was relevant, because his pride and joy was the herd of fighting bulls he kept on his 2,000-acre farm. He grew sunflowers, wheat and barley but the land was really too dry for such crops, especially the year we were there, which was in the middle of a drought, and the crops did not look well.

But his bulls looked fine and he was proud to show them off to us. He was speculating whether six of his animals might be selected for the next Cordoba event that he said was one of the most prestigious in Spain.

Later he performance-tested some of the young heifers in the herd in his own corrida built for the purpose. It looked like the real deal, with him swinging a cape and wielding a toy wooden sword, except that the animals were half grown and female. He explained that it was not possible to test the bulls because that would ruin them for any real bullfight. But testing the heifers to find out how aggressive they were at a young age gave a clue as to what kind of bull they might produce later in life.

He was a fascinating man. Larger than life but gentle and loving to his large family. And on the farm he rode a superb Andalusian filly, one of which he used for playing polo. What a character. But we did not learn much about his views on the EU. There was too much else to talk to him about.

Another larger-than-life character was Anthony Gurney, remember him? He and I were members of a party that visited Romania in 1976 to look at agriculture under the communist dictator, Ceausescu.

It was organised by a Norfolk man called Derek Bickford Smith who had been a salesman for BOCM and was the first time most of us had been behind the iron curtain. We were taken round huge state farms and cooperatives with large herds of cattle and pigs and growing sub-standard crops. I remember vividly walking onto a field of potatoes and finding an infestation of Colorado beetles. In Britain, at the time, a sighting of one such beetle was enough to declare a national emergency. But the Romanians didn't seem to notice except when we all emptied the turn-ups of our trousers when we left the field.

The commissar looking after us was called Georgescu, and one evening he took over what appeared like a nightclub to provide us with dinner. When you were a commissar in Romania you could do things like that. He retained the cooking staff and the waiters, of course, and some dodgy looking characters on the stage playing zithers and other instruments for our entertainment. Anyway, it was Anthony's turn to do a vote of thanks and at the end of the evening, during which the food had been almost inedible, he stood up to speak.

And in his ex-Indian army voice he said (and this all had to be translated as he said it), "Well done George. You've shown us some marvellous farms, some marvellous herds of cows and pigs and now you've brought us here for this hospitality which I'm bound to say was – different. When I came over here on the aeroplane I bought a bottle of duty-free scotch that I was going to give you. I hid it behind that radiator over there but when I went to fetch it just now it had gorn. I expect those jonnies in the band must have nicked it. Never mind. Well done George."

Lorna and I led a party for Field Farm Tours starting in St Petersburg, where we got our second look at the paintings and treasures in the Summer Palace, among other things, then travelled by train through forests to the northern border of Finland. From Finland we crossed to Sweden by overnight ferry and finally took a bus into Norway. That was a memorable tour.

En route we stayed in Helsinki for a couple of nights. In passing I should mention that Helsinki was the cleanest capital city I had ever been in. There was no graffiti, no litter. It was a real pleasure to walk the streets. I felt ashamed of the state of some UK cities and wondered what foreign visitors thought of them.

As leaders, Lorna and I were often treated to the best room. We didn't ask for it and it was embarrassing when it happened, but that was the way it was. And the Helsinki hotel down by the waterside was one of those occasions. We were shown up to the room on the top floor by a concierge and he proudly pointed out all its features. There was a king-size bed, a fridge full of liquor and mixer drinks, a bathroom with a glass window dividing it from the bedroom and the pièce de résistance – a mirror on the ceiling. I can't say we made much use of the mirror but it was there if we wanted it.

When our three children were in their teens, Lorna and I decided to take them to Holland and Denmark in our car. One reason was to drop Andrew, our eldest, off at a farm in Holland to stay for a couple of months with some farming friends we had made over there on a previous trip, and the rest of us, me, Lorna, Rob and Fiona (who would have been fifteen and thirteen), then carried on through Schleswig-Holstein to Denmark. I had some people I wanted to see on the way to inform myself on certain aspects of Danish agriculture and we were booked to come back to England on the car ferry from Esbjerg.

We enjoyed our tour through Denmark, visiting more friends on the way, and arrived at Esbjerg a little too early for the ferry. We had an hour or so to kill so I decided to find the beach that I knew from past experience you could drive on. We sat there in the car with the wind whistling around the car, watching the big waves that had built up as they crossed the Atlantic, crash onto the sand. Then another car pulled up alongside us. And we all watched the waves together. Suddenly all the doors on the other car opened at once and two adults and two teenage children stripped off all their clothes and ran, naked into the sea. The mother was a bit delayed because she had to find her bathing hat. Having found it she pulled it on her head and followed her family into the waves. The Danes are uninhibited that way – apparently.

We led a tour to Italy and Carolyne Cree, who had, by then, succeeded Jill Lewis as managing director of Field Farm Tours, coinciding with the change of name from AgriTravel, found a man to act as our English-speaking guide. He wasn't a professional guide. He was more into AI – artificial insemination not artificial intelligence – but he knew a lot of people and put together an interesting tour. We went to a Parmesan cheese dairy, a butchery producing prosciutto (uncooked ham for the uninitiated) and of course to his AI farm.

We went to Naples, and to see the Vesuvius volcano, which fortunately was not erupting at the time but had obliterated Pompeii by covering it with volcanic ash in AD 79. Walking around the excavated ruins of Pompeii was an education in how advanced the Romans were 2,000 years ago.

But our guide also booked us into a farm-based hotel, which was nice in some ways but it was made up of converted farm buildings. This had the disadvantage of rooms of different standards, which can cause problems in a group where everyone is paying the same price. One lovely middle-aged lady with us was a widow, so was travelling alone and she was allocated a room in a converted look-out tower high above the farmyard. I had a habit of scribbling lots of limericks about things that happened on all the tours we did and reading them out after dinner on the last night. This is what I wrote about her:

Our Joan had a room in the sky
To watch all the men passing by.
They went up her stairs
In singles and pairs,
Came down with a satisfied sigh.

It wasn't true, of course, but it raised a laugh and Joan took it in good part.

I wrote one such verse about an elderly lady who came to Cuba with us. It suggested that one evening, when we went to see a show called Tropicana in Havana, she had, perhaps, overindulged on the rum and coke. I used to type the verses when I got home and send them to all participants as a keepsake of the tour. On the Saturday morning after I had posted the Cuban lot, my phone rang quite early.

It was the elderly lady who said, "I've just opened my post and read your poem. Tell me, are you going to publish it in the *Farmers Weekly*?" I replied that, no, I was not intending to publish it and added, "You had to be there to appreciate it." To which she said, "Good, because if you do I shall sue." And she put the phone down. I didn't publish and we made friends again afterwards. But you'll have noticed, I still haven't identified her.

One of our first skiing holidays was to Arosa, one of the best ski resorts in Switzerland. There was a party of about ten of us – all Norfolk farmers and wives. The snow that year was perfect because there had been a heavy fall the week before we arrived. Our skiing abilities were mixed so we would all go off in the morning either to ski class or free skiing, and then meet for lunch in one of the mountain restaurants.

The main topic of conversation between us that year was slurry. One of our number, Jimmy, who was a dairy farmer, had invented a machine to separate the liquids from the solids in cow slurry by squeezing it through a kind of sieve, then collecting the results separately. It made so much sense. You could then pump the liquid element and store it in a tank and stack the solids for mechanical spreading on the land later.

Such machines are commonplace now. Few dairy farms are without one. But Jimmy's was the first, the prototype, which set the standard for those that followed. And he was anxious to hear our views on the design, on patenting it, on who he might sell the idea to, about marketing the concept and so on. It was a discussion that lasted the whole two weeks despite protestations from our wives. And it occurred to me that it was a paradox to be spending our time talking about a rather disgusting subject in such a pristine environment.

Recently I have retired from leading tours and taken up more leisurely pursuits, such as cruising. And since I lost my dear wife, Lorna, in 2018 I have been travelling with Jill Lewis; the same Jill who used to arrange all my tours. We enjoy one another's company; we both love to travel and look at the odd farm when possible, so it suits us both admirably.

A year or two ago we went on a River Danube cruise. It was very enjoyable. Lots of wonderful scenery alongside the river, sightseeing stops in interesting places, and a boat with not too many passengers so you could get to know other travellers. Jill and I were sitting having a drink one evening and speaking to some people who had sat next to us when a small lady came over and said, "Excuse me interrupting, but are you David Richardson?" I gave my usual noncommitting reply saying, "I've been told I look like him." To which she said, "So why have you got his voice?" She had, in fact, been eavesdropping the conversation I'd been having, and recognised my voice from when I did regular radio programmes many years before.

She was Liz Russell who was on the cruise with her husband, Archie. She recognised my voice because she was a dairy farmer's daughter from Lancashire and she owned a company called Envirobed. One of the main things she produced and which had given her company its name was bedding for cows derived from discarded newspapers. And among her other products was a powder that could be scattered on the bedding of any kind of farm animal – cows and horses in particular – that would virtually eliminate the liquids in their dung. We spent a long time with Liz and Archie after that, talking about the merits of such products and have since become firm friends. And once again I was discussing faeces in an inappropriate environment. I suppose I must have a dirty mind.

EPILOGUE

To those who have come new to these memoirs and to those who have accompanied me on my travels and added to my pleasure: I hope you've enjoyed travelling with me through these pages as much as I have in remembering what good times we had.

If fellow travellers think I have remembered some details wrongly, I apologise. I probably have. Some of my old records of early tours and excursions were lost in a house move some years ago and others were stored on the floor in a damp room and totally spoiled. I have therefore relied almost totally on my memories of places and events, so if details are not totally accurate or if I have missed some key events, I'm sorry and it is my fault. But what you have read is what my memory told me happened and that's all I can say.

I want to take this opportunity to thank again all those who have shared these experiences with me. You know who you are and please take this as my expression of gratitude for your friendship. I won't name many names but I must thank in particular my dear friend, and these days, travelling companion, Jill Lewis. It has been a constant joy working with her over the years as we planned dozens of tours together and I am so pleased we are still in constant contact. And Carolyne Cree, who took over where Jill left off. Carolyne has been a worthy successor and has continued to run Field Farm Tours as the friendly customer-focused business it always was, even when it had a different name.

I don't travel so much these days. The legs have gone, and while the spirit is strong the flesh is weak. But when I do, I think of what we did together and smile.

Adieu

Jill Lewis and Ben Nevis

David is also author of 'In at the Deep End'

"David Richardson is a veteran farmer, businessman and communicator whose skills have been · recognised over the years by both peers and admirers. During more than 50 years of writing and broadcasting about farming, food and the countryside he has earned a reputation for straight talking and common sense. His analyses of rural issues are uncompromising. His criticisms of officialdom are penetrating and his recognition and exposure of humbug are instinctive and incisive."

Available on Amazon scan the QR code to buy the book

TRICORN
BOOKS